THE SWORD
AND THE CROSS

BBC Scotland

THE SWORD AND THE CROSS

Four Turbulent Episodes in the History of Christian Scotland

Introduced by
RICHARD HOLLOWAY

SAINT ANDREW PRESS
Edinburgh

First published in 2003 by
SAINT ANDREW PRESS
121 George Street
Edinburgh EH2 4YN

Text copyright © BBC Scotland, 2003
By arrangement with the BBC
The BBC logo is a registered trademark of the British Broadcasting Corporation
and is used under licence
BBC logo © BBC 1996
Introduction © Richard Holloway, 2003
The Scots Confession of Faith translation by James Bulloch © The Church of Scotland

ISBN 0 7152 0809 8

The authorial views expressed in this book are those of the authors alone.
The opinions expressed by the authors and their interviewees do not represent the
official views of the Church of Scotland, which can be laid down only by the
General Assembly.

British Library Cataloguing in Publication Data
A catalogue record for this book is available from the British Library

Typeset by Waverley Typesetters, Galashiels
Printed and bound in the United Kingdom by The Bath Press

CONTENTS

'The Killing Times': as Charles II tightened his grip on the Covenanters, the most faithful of them slipped through his fingers and into the hills.
Photograph: David Quinn

INTRODUCTION

RICHARD HOLLOWAY

Since they started talking, human beings have been telling stories to try to explain themselves to themselves. By using your imagination, you can almost get into the heads of our early ancestors as self-consciousness started firing into life in their brains. There they were in their caves and forests, looking out onto life with all its baffling necessities, and questions start flickering across their emerging minds: Who are we? Where did we come from? Are we alone? Is there anybody there? That's when the stories started coming – and they've been coming ever since.

Before it got pushed off the bestseller list a few years ago, the big story in Scotland was Christianity. For better or for worse, the Christian story formed our nation's history, and to understand Scotland today you have to know something of that story and feel its power. It is a drama of original innocence

and its ancient loss. It's about our fall from grace and our wandering in the far country of hopelessness. It is also about One who comes to rescue us, to bring us back from exile. The Christian story is one of the most dramatic stories ever told, yet there is something so frightening about it that it can paralyse us with anxiety, because it tells us that the meaning and peace we crave is found only after death in the life to come. This life is a brief prelude to that other life, which will last forever, either as an eternity of bliss or as an eternity of loss and torment. It is not surprising, therefore, that when it was believed in its entirety this story had the power to terrify monarchs, convulse nations and drive men and women into desert places or onto islands at the edge of the world to prepare themselves for the final judgement of God. It is a story that provoked selfless love and unbridled hatred; overwhelming pity and implacable cruelty; greatness of soul and suffocating bigotry; crippling superstition and liberating honesty. It is the story of Christian Scotland.

One of the things we know about stories is that they have a life of their own. That is why history is a two-way street, in which a story from the past can impose itself like a living virus on the present and profoundly and damagingly affect the way we live and think right now. We only have to think of the continuing effect on some Scottish football supporters of the ugly conflict between Protestantism and Catholicism that for so long disfigured the life of our nation, a topic which was looked at in considerable depth in the television series on which this book is based. But as well as feeling the continuing impact of the past on attitudes today, we can reverse the process and read the preoccupations of our own time back into the past, in order to provide them with some sort of respectable pedigree. Historians call this phenomenon 'retrojection', and a good example is provided in our own time by the Celtic Spirituality industry, which claims the support of Saint Columba for many laudable but entirely contemporary enthusiasms. In fact, the closer you get to the historical Columba the more alien and frightening he becomes. In that, he is a lot like Jesus himself, on whose example Adomnan seems to have modelled his celebrated life of the great Scottish saint. History never repeats itself, but we always do.

To measure the full impact of Christianity on Scotland, you have to go back thousands of years before Columba landed on Iona, back to the history of ancient Israel. It is certainly not possible to understand the Scottish Reformation – the great revolution of 1560 that separated Scottish Christianity from 1,000 years of its history and set up a new Kirk – without knowing something about that wandering tribe of Semites who founded an uneasy little kingdom 3,000 years ago on a tiny sliver of territory at the eastern edge of the Mediterranean that we still call the Holy Land. This is not just because Christianity is the daughter who ran away from her Jewish home, married a Gentile and started her own family; it is also because some of the reformers in the sixteenth century saw the times they were living through as a re-enactment of the life of that ancient and troubled kingdom. The Jews saw themselves as a people who had been specially chosen by God. They sometimes used the metaphor of marriage: God had married himself to Israel, had made a covenant with her. He would be her God, would be faithful to her; and she would be his people and be true to him. When the Hebrew historians wrote down the history of their people hundreds of years later, in what Christians call the Old Testament, they used this idea of the covenant between God and Israel as a key to interpret what had happened. The story they told was of God's constant faithfulness and Israel's constant unfaithfulness. Again and again, God warned his bride to be true to him. Again and again, we read that Israel committed adultery by going after other gods until, finally, God could endure it no more and banished her forever.

That ancient story of the broken covenant between Israel and God is a fundamental key to understanding the spiritual and psychological landscape of the Reformation and the troubled centuries that followed it. The Reformation was a muddle of dirty politics and opportunistic greed, inter-mixed with the genuine spiritual agony of some extraordinary people. To understand it, we must remind ourselves of the momentous claim that Christianity made for itself: it offered men and women the possibility of eternal bliss or eternal woe. If men and women were faithful to their covenant with God, a glorious and unending future awaited them in heaven. But the price of infidelity was unending torment, graphically depicted in those Doom paintings that were inscribed in such horrifying detail above the chancel arches of medieval churches. Was the great medieval Catholic Church, with its glorious splendour and its scarlet sins, any longer the pure Bride of Christ? Or had she become the great whore who had run after other gods and forfeited her place in the eternal habitations?

That question burned in the mind of Martin Luther, the great German Reformer who lit the fuse to the explosion that convulsed Europe and changed forever the face of Western history. As he read the Bible in his monastic cell, agonising over whether or not he would be saved, Luther had an epiphany. We were not saved by our works, our prayers and pilgrimages, our masses and indulgences; we were not even saved by our good deeds; we were saved only by the grace of God. We were justified not by anything in our humanity, which was as filthy rags, but only by our faith in the mercy of God. We should trust in that alone, he suddenly realised, not in church or pope or any other human agency. That event in Luther's mind was one of the great turning points of human history. It might even be seen as the birth of the modern individual, the soul standing naked before God. Luther's epiphany was an inner surrender to an absolute truth: his helplessness and God's overwhelming grace. A possible analogy might be the moment when an alcoholic reaches absolute rock bottom – 'the gutter', to use the language of AA – admits absolute helplessness and reaches out to the possibility of change through a day-at-a-time life of trust in a higher power. However we think of it, that moment in Luther's cell set off a tidal wave of change that rushed over Europe. With its final surge, it hit Scotland and swept away the ancient Catholic Church of this land.

Historians have noticed that the later the Reformation hit a country, the more radical it was. That was certainly the way it worked in Scotland. When I was taught Church history, of the sectarian Episcopalian variety, my tutor used a homely metaphor to get his point across. He said that if a wee boy came home to his mother with a filthy face, she could do any of three things: she could leave his face dirty; she could wash his face thoroughly; or she could cut off his head. That piece of breezy oversimplification was meant to capture the three main responses to the great challenge that confronted the Church in the sixteenth century. The Catholic Church did nothing – it just left the wee boy's face dirty; the Anglican and Lutheran Churches cleaned the wee boy up; but the Calvinist Churches lopped off the boy's head and adopted another child instead. There's enough truth in the metaphor to make it dangerously useful.

Photograph:
David Quinn

Institutional Catholicism held out too long against the legitimate challenge to its compromises and corruptions to save Christendom, but it had its own clean-up later in what came to be known as the Counter-Reformation. It is also true that Anglicanism and Lutheranism kept more of the old ethos around, including bishops and something of the colour of the old Christian calendar of feasts and fasts. But when the Reformation finally took in Scotland, it saw the complete death of the old order and the birth of something very new and different. That may be because one of its agents was a man called John Knox. This book takes a fresh look at Knox, who is so central to Scotland's self-understanding, and attempts to uncover the man behind the myth. In making the television series on which this book is based, I really encountered Knox for the first time. He's not my type, but it is impossible not to have at least a grudging respect for this tormented figure.

At Knox's funeral, the Earl of Morton described him as a man 'who never feared' – but it is hard to agree with that assessment. Fear seems to have been an important ingredient in his personality, and it may be the key to his character. After all, the brave man is not the man who never feels fear, but the man who feels it and overcomes it. Knox's complex character suggests that he had a lifelong struggle with fear, and much of it was spiritual. His conversion to Protestantism was so deep and radical, it persuaded him that he was engaged in spiritual warfare against enemies with whom there could be no compromise. It is difficult to figure out whether the apocalyptic theology he espoused gave the harsh edge to his personality, or whether it was a case of an already obdurate personality finding a theology that suited it. It may be too facile a thing to say, but I suspect that a certain inner fearfulness might have caused him to

over-compensate by developing a fierce and uncompromising style. There is no doubt that there was a pattern of flight from danger throughout his career; but there was also the final emergence of a flinty consistency in him that is not unlike the demeanour of the Old Testament prophets he revered. Something of that quality inhered in the Kirk he did so much to root among the Scottish people. And as a final and illuminating irony, it is worth noting that the author of *The First Blast of the Trumpet against the Monstrous Regiment of Women* left instructions that his young wife and their three daughters were to be the executors of his will.

Whatever the truth of Knox's character, the Scottish Reformation swept away every vestige of what Philip Larkin called 'that vast, moth-eaten musical brocade' of medieval Christianity. With it, until within living memory, went much of the colour and closeness to nature that was inherited from the old paganism, and which had been tactfully baptised into Christianity by Catholicism. And with all of that went Catholicism's rueful tolerance of human weakness, and its genial and not-so-genial corruptions. Of course, none of this happened overnight. The revolution of 1560 was not completed until the Covenanters won their struggle against the Stuart monarchs at the end of the following century. The Stuarts tried to tailor the Reformed Scottish Kirk to their own refined tastes. They overreached themselves and fell, opening the way for the establishment of the effective theocratic rigour of the new Kirk, which inculcated discipline and promoted a new kind of literate culture that ran counter to many of the old human weaknesses and cravings – and by the same dynamic created new, perhaps more powerfully entrenched psychological weaknesses. In time, it promoted a type of Scottish personality that was thrawn, argumentative, defiantly suspicious of all systems of power and enduringly incorruptible. The success of the Reformation project makes a decadent like me shiver and thank God that he came along when it was on its last legs. Even so, though it does not warm my heart, the achievement of the Scottish Reformation was formidable and made us, if not what we are today, certainly what we were yesterday.

Scottish Christianity, so far, has been a drama in three acts: Columba and the gradual formation of Catholic Scotland; Knox and the Great Breaking from that past; and the return of Catholicism and its increasing prominence in the land that rejected it so fiercely 500 years before. One of the saddest chapters in the history of the Church of Scotland was its racist response to the Irish immigrants who started pouring into the West of Scotland in the late nineteenth century. The malignant residue of that campaign against Irish Catholics is still with us in the sectarianism that is still such a feature of life in certain sections of Scottish society. But the comforting thing to note is that the Catholic Church in Scotland today is a strong and self-confident institution that plays a significant part in the life of the nation that sent it packing centuries ago.

While the revival of Catholicism may be cheering, the news for Scottish Christianity as a whole at the beginning of the twenty-first century is depressing. Since the 1960s, the story has been one of unhalting decline. In fact, the haemorrhage of members is so serious that sociologists talk confidently about the death of Christianity in the not-too-distant future. Well, Christianity is an anvil that has worn out many hammers in the past; but there is no doubt that the churches in Scotland today could be described as simply another set of voluntary associations in the midst of an increasingly secular and multicultural nation. The good news is that they no longer fight among themselves. In fact, it is probably true to say that they are now a bit too inclined to keep quiet about the significant disagreements that still divide them. In the face of an increasingly secular Scottish culture, maybe they have found that the things they have in common are more important than the things that separate them. And it is just possible that, in their weakened state, they may finally learn the lesson that Jesus tried to teach them 2,000 years ago: 'By this everyone will know that you are my disciples, if you have love for one another.'

RICHARD HOLLOWAY

PART 1

COLUMBA

WARRIOR ABBOT

Iona.
Photograph: Joyce Watson

Prologue

By the middle of the ninth century, relentless Viking raids along Scotland's shores had driven deep into the ancient territories of the Gaels and the Picts. Their homelands had been ripped apart and the inhabitants forced to flee. But from this chaos would rise a new kingdom – the nation that we now call Scotland. And it would owe its birth to a religious faith that would utterly transform this once pagan land: Christianity.

Many of the Gaels of the Inner Hebrides and west coast chose to move inland, with their King, Kenneth MacAlpin. Following his final defeat of the Picts, he united the warring tribes to forge a brand new kingdom. But uniting Scotland was not something that he could have done alone. He owed his authority over his new subjects to a tiny box of bones – the sacred remains of a long-dead monk named Columba, one of history's most mysterious and shadowy figures.

Columba's bones symbolised something new, and historically momentous – the binding of kings with the Christian faith. Thanks to Columba, Scotland's subjects looked to their king as defender of their spiritual well-being as well as their physical well-being. The Church became the cornerstone of Kenneth MacAlpin's rule, and Christianity went on to shape Scotland for over 1,000 years.

This is the extraordinary story of how Columba conferred power on the kings of Scotland and changed forever the history of the nation. Across the centuries since that time, the turbulent relationship between Church and State – sometimes inspiring, often bloody, always dramatic – *is* the story of Christian Scotland.

But to uncover the truth about the origins of Scottish Christianity and its roots in the life and work of Scotland's first patron saint, we must go beyond historical fact-finding. We must examine the astonishing power of the spoken and written word over centuries, and decipher a series of ancient riddles left by those who followed in Columba's footsteps.

A handful of his followers left us stories and poems about Columba's life. We have vague fragments in Irish Annals. However, most of what we know about him is contained in his biography, written after his death by Adomnan, the ninth Abbot of the monastery that Columba founded on the Hebridean island of Iona.

The first mystery to be solved is one that is key to interpreting Columba's life. It is the question of why he left Ireland – his home and the centre of the thriving Gaelic kingdom of Dalriada – to come to Iona.

Iona.
Photograph: Joyce Watson

Disgrace and Departure (AD 563)

In the sixth century AD, the north of Ireland was the heartland of the Gaelic kingdom of Dalriada. It was a society dominated by two feuding families: the southern and northern Ui Neill. If you were anybody in this society, you belonged to one or the other – and if you belonged to one, you would, sooner or later, find yourself at war with the other. These two dynasties maintained a brutal balance of power and commanded ferocious family loyalties.

Life at this time was nasty, brutish and short. Death was always very close. Society was warlike, and people asserted their strength by going into battle, even against their own kin. Self-styled kings and warlords abounded. There were laws, but whether you actually got justice depended on how many 'heavies' you had on your side. Straying from your own territory was ill-advised, unless you had the blessing of the local warlords, as well as some trusted bodyguards.

It was into this violent, dynastic society that Columba was born in AD 521, not as a member of one of the many downtrodden families who ran for cover at every Ui Neill feud, but as a high-ranking member of the northern Ui Neill aristocracy. He was no less than a prince; a contender for the very highest rank in this warlord society: king.

The warrior aristocracy into which he was born inhabited a world in which power was built on wealth and weaponry: how much did you have and how much could you get by force of arms? Columba's kin commanded the best, most tight-knit and successful men of violence in Ireland.

Little archaeological evidence from this period remains but it is clear that, for those at the bottom of the social pyramid, life in this society was very brutal indeed. For the elite, however, it had its compensations. This was a kingdom, after all, that crafted fine artefacts from expensive materials imported from the Mediterranean, the Middle East and Asia.

Far from being part of a distant Celtic 'fringe', the kingdom of Dalriada was in the mainstream of European culture. And of all the continental sophistications that had made their way across the sea, perhaps the most significant was an exotic religion called Christianity. Its adherents dressed differently, and had new technologies like writing. To the people of Dalriada, they must have seemed as strange and bizarre as aliens. It was clear that these new 'Christians' had some kind of power – and the people of Irish Dalriada could buy into that power by converting to Christianity.

Christianity had come to Ireland from distant Rome, via Britain. But while its roots had spread into most of Britain, Roman influence had petered out in the northern land that the Romans called Caledonia and that we now call Scotland. Northern Britain at that time was a tribal mix of Gaels, Britons and Picts. The Romans found it difficult to implant their culture fully and successfully: in the end, they had had to settle for simply occupying the territory.

Earlier, in the first century AD, Rome had looked set to conquer Caledonia, a brooding land of mountain and forest, but when things at home began to go wrong, the Romans dropped their plans to push the Empire further northwards. After all, the land to the north was hardly a glittering prize; range after range of dark hills populated by a savage mixture of hostile tribes. Compared with Rome, the weather was atrocious, the hosts were unwelcoming and the food was terrible. They retreated to their defensive line at Hadrian's Wall, and the Roman brand of Christianity ventured no further north.

Instead, Christianity moved westwards across the Irish Sea. St Patrick arrived in the northern part of Ireland in the early fifth century, and sowed the seeds of this powerful new form of spirituality despite initial hostility. He described having to pay bodyguards to accompany him. But despite the opposition of some of the nobility, people began converting to Christianity. This new religion was a novelty, and attracted young people especially, perhaps as a form of Dark Age 'teenage rebellion'.

Christianity had a genius for punctuating the ordinary grind of human existence with feast and festival, but it was also ideally suited to the kind of society in which life was a constant struggle against the elements. It was a drama of salvation that conferred meaning on even the harshest life. Christianity was a faith that gave strength and a sense of permanence to mortals coping with a cold, brutal world. And into this way of living stepped a remarkable and complex figure: Columba.

From the scant evidence we have, it would appear that, by the time Columba was born, Christianity had already taken root in this turbulent Gaelic society. Columba, himself, seems to have had no choice where Christianity was concerned – at his birth he was fostered to a priest. Fostership was common practice among the Dalriadan nobility, but it was relatively rare to be fostered to the Church.

We know little of Columba's physical appearance. Some sources suggest he was short and powerfully built. Events suggest that he was prone to furious tempers. Personal charisma seems to have emerged to complement his highly distinguished lineage.

Columba.

Nor was the education he received wasted on a feeble intellect. Scriptural training and a passion for books – an exclusively Christian form of 'information technology' in an age virtually without writing – marked him out. The scant information we have suggests that, by early adulthood, he was becoming a successful missionary.

With his noble lineage, sharp intellect and the powerful spiritual cachet of being Christian, Columba's reputation as a holy man grew. A prince by birth, and, by training, a sophisticated and highly educated priest, he was clearly destined for great things. Yet, at the height of his power and influence, something happened that resulted in a spectacular fall from grace, culminating in his exile from Ireland.

The trouble began in AD 561. Adomnan's biography does not detail exactly what Columba did. We are left with a series of tantalising leads from fragmented sources, all of which have one thing in common: they utterly overturn the popular image of the mild-mannered saint.

Piecing together the sequence of events that engulfed Columba at this time is largely informed guesswork, but it seems that his passion for books may have got him into more trouble than he could possibly have imagined. One version of the story tells that, during a visit to his old tutor, the abbot, Finnian, Columba took the opportunity to shut himself away at night with Finnian's *Book of Psalms*. Under the cloak of darkness, he copied it – without Finnian's permission.

To understand why this would set in train the disastrous sequence of events that it did we have to see this act through the eyes of sixth-century people. In an age when reading and writing were treasured gifts of learning and tools of political power, the copying of a text was no trivial crime. Books had not been part of the pre-Christian Gaelic world, and they must have inspired a sense of awe. Books – and their contents – were of incalculable value.

Finnian, so the story goes, was outraged that Columba had duplicated his book and demanded to have the copy that Columba had made. When Columba refused to hand it over, Diarmaid, High King and chief of Columba's enemies, the southern Ui Neill, was called upon to decide the matter.

Diarmaid's judgement left no room for doubt: 'To every cow its calf, to every book its copy'. One of the earliest cases of breach of copyright had been settled. Columba had to hand over his copy of the Psalms. However, it is strongly implied that instead of meekly accepting the judgement, Columba was deeply resentful. And what followed next tipped him from resentment into fury.

A youth on the run from High King Diarmaid sought refuge with Columba. It was a perfectly rational course of action – respect for Columba's spiritual status should have ensured the boy's safety. Instead of sparing the youth, however, Diarmaid had the boy wrenched from the sanctuary of Columba's presence and killed.

Diarmaid had gone too far. Judging against Columba in the copying scandal had been one thing, but now the High King had transgressed a boundary of huge significance by undermining Columba's priestly authority.

The fragments of the story that we have suggest that Columba's thoughts immediately turned to vengeance, and that he sped home to rally the forces of his close kin, the northern Ui Neill, against High King Diarmaid's southern Ui Neill. What followed was no minor skirmish. At Cul Drebene in AD 561, they engaged in one of the biggest and most bloody battles of their time.

The amassing armies of clansmen numbered several thousand on each side. At first, the southern Ui Neill enjoyed the advantage of fog which allowed them to approach, while remaining invisible to the northerners. But then, as if by a miracle, the fog lifted, and the northerners launched their attack. The battle was savage. No prisoners were taken; there was no medical support and no mercy. The level of casualties must have been appalling. But the northern Ui Neill were, finally, victorious.

Something else happened at Cul Drebene, however, that shocked both sides, and appalled even Columba's admirers. As if being the cause of the battle was not bad enough, it is also suggested that Columba, himself, was in the thick of the action. Cryptic mentions of a prominent scar appear repeatedly in Adomnan's chronicle. It is curious that this physical feature is

commented on so often. Where could a holy man, such as Columba, have obtained such a scar? It may be that, as the conflict boiled over at Cul Drebene, Columba was drawn in. He may have swung his *own* bloodstained sword in this savage battle. If so, his spiritual credentials would, understandably, have been tarnished.

There is, however, another interpretation from different sources, which, at first, appears to be less damaging. In this version of events, Columba did not actually fight, but simply *prayed* for victory for his close kin, the northern Ui Neill.

To the modern, secular mind, this may seem a less damning accusation than that of wielding a sword; but this was the sixth century, and men of spiritual power like Columba were believed to exert supernatural influence over events – influence well beyond the power of ordinary men. If Columba had prayed for his kin's victory in battle, it would certainly have been seen as a misuse of that spiritual influence. Whether it took the form of public prayer, ritual, or blessing of his own warriors, it would have been interpreted as a betrayal of what Christianity was supposed to be about. Columba was praying for violent men who achieved their ends by killing people. At the very least, it would have fuelled the fire of his enemies' wrath.

So, from the history, what can we piece together about Columba's character? Columba, the defiant thief? Columba the blood-spattered warrior-priest? or Columba the abuser of spiritual authority?

Photograph: David Quinn

These were the 'Dark Ages', and we will never know the whole truth – but what is in no doubt from the sources we do have is that Columba's glittering career in the Church juddered to a halt.

A synod of the Irish Church was assembled after the battle of Cul Drebene. What were they to do with the miscreant, Columba? The problem for Columba was that the synod was held on Diarmaid's home territory, and, with the synod under the High King's influence, the outcome was probably inescapable. They excommunicated Columba.

Excommunication was a devastating penalty, an ecclesiastical banishment that could be likened to being in the desert without water. It was a terrible price for Columba to pay, and it did not matter that it was revoked almost immediately – the damage had been done.

Columba had disgraced himself within his own tight-knit community. Immediately he sought to make amends. And he did it through a practice that was the very backbone of early Christian life: *penance.*

A combination of confession and voluntary self-denial, penance was a key way of expressing what was, and was not, acceptable to Christians. By this process, those who had sinned and damaged their relationship with their Church and community could be restored to some kind of wholeness. The extent of the sin was measured, calibrated by the Church, and the penance undertaken reflected the seriousness of the sin. Columba's penance was 'white martyrdom'. He had to become a 'pilgrim for Christ'. This particular form of martyrdom was designed to take a man away from his kin and country; and from his rights and privileges.

He had to leave Ireland, and this he did within two years of the Battle of Cul Drebene. It meant letting go of everything in his homeland that mattered to him. He had once been a contender for the position of High King, and his prospects in Ireland had been golden. Now Columba would have to start his life all over again. At the age of 41, he had to leave behind the security of close kin and the privilege of royal status for an uncertain future.

Columba's True Achievement

From the sanctuary of his powerful family in Irish Dalriada, Columba and a handful of companions set out to sea. However, although the penance he was undertaking involved an element of banishment, Columba's destination was no obscure foreign continent. It was merely a distant corner of the same Gaelic kingdom of his homeland. For Dalriada was a sea kingdom, and it extended north and east from Irish Dalriada across dangerous waters to its northern half, Scottish Dalriada – the part of Scotland we now know as Argyll.

Iona.

The sea routes between Irish and Scottish Dalriada were an important means of communication in Columba's day, and they were well travelled. The Gaels of both areas were closely related: they spoke the same language, and many aspects of their lives were similar. Our view of the Scottish Highlands today might lead us to expect that Scottish Dalriada was an isolated community, but far from being on the periphery, the sea-lanes were the motorways of their day, making travel between Irish and Scottish Dalriada quick and efficient.

But, accessible though Scottish Dalriada might have been, many drowned on the crossings. The waters between the north of Ireland and Columba's eventual destination of Iona are hazardous, and sailing these waters in the

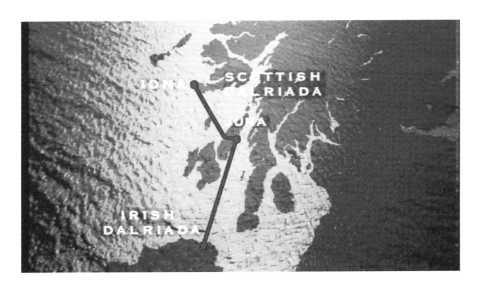

Columba's likely route from Irish Dalriada to Iona.

kind of small wood and leather craft available to Columba would have been extremely dangerous.

Recent research, however, points to a unique safe route for Columba's voyage from Ireland to Iona. This research has shown that, by passing through a key way-point, Columba would have been able to avoid the worst Atlantic gales and the treacherous waters of the southern Hebrides. This new theory suggests that Columba's route to Iona passed over a narrow land-corridor between two sea lochs on the island of Jura. Following a known, direct sea route from Ireland to the island of Islay, the boat would have arrived on the east coast of Jura. It would have been carried across land for a short distance, and then navigated through the sheltered sea loch, Loch Tarbert, out to the west coast, well away from the deep Atlantic swells. From there, it was only a short, and relatively safe, sea journey to the island of Colonsay and from there to Iona.

Also on Jura, there is a classic landing cross. When a boat landed, grateful travellers would have taken a stone, inscribed it, and placed a cross on it, as thanks to God for a successful landing. This would also have served as a potential landmark for future travellers.

Columba's crossing was an act of considerable physical courage, but it was also a parable of his Christian faith. The Bible had taught him that he was an exile on Earth, far from his heavenly homeland. By turning his back on his beloved Ireland, he was acting out his faith.

Reaching the end of his journey, however, would have given him and his companions cold comfort. There was much work to be done. Iona was little more than a wild, wave-battered rock. Columba and his brothers now found themselves on an un-inhabited island, with nothing to eat, no shelter, few building materials and a challenging climate. This harsh place would be where he would live his life of penance. But first, Columba and his companions had to survive. They built rudimentary huts, and began ploughing the land in order to have crops for the following year. Locals on Mull gave them the occasional gift to keep them going, but they had to find food wherever they

*Stone used as a landmark
and symbol of gratitude
for a safe arrival.*

Iona.

could. There were seal-breeding grounds nearby, and they 'harvested' seals for food. They could not afford to be sentimental about the animal world.

Iona promised a grim, hand-to-mouth existence, but the harsh environment was not their only problem. This island was 'sword-land' – disputed territory on a volatile border. It was a dangerous no-man's-land between two warring tribes: the Gaels, who shared their culture with Columba's Irish homeland, and the savage Picts who dominated inland Scotland. No sane person would have chosen to live on Iona.

But, happily, Columba and his fellows were not hacked to pieces. At the time of their arrival, Iona was controlled, not by the hostile Picts, but

Photograph: Joyce Watson

by locals who had a lot in common with Columba. The inhabitants of nearby Mull and the mainland welcomed Columba as a spiritual visitor because they were not only fellow Gaelic-speaking Dalriadians, but also Christians themselves.

For a few seeds of Christianity had already been sown in Scotland before Columba arrived on these shores. Contrary to one of the most persistent popular myths, Columba was not the first person to bring Christianity to Scotland. Traders from the east would have passed on the new Christian beliefs, and, although there had been no concerted effort to convert Caledonia, a few Roman missionaries had ventured north.

The Roman border was by no means watertight, and a frontier version of Christianity had filtered through. But, far from the controlling influence of the Roman Church, what had emerged was a form of Christianity that had

learned to co-exist with the pagan rituals of the indigenous tribes. It existed only in isolated pockets, and had mutated far from its origins.

Columba's task – to establish a Christian heartland in this context – was a colossal undertaking. Yet, somehow, within thirty years, he had created a community of monasteries that became a bright beacon of Christianity, and an influential part of the Church.

The key to Columba's improbable achievement lay in the skills he had learned back in Ireland – the skills of a politician.

Columba might have taken on a life of penance to bring himself closer to God, but princely blood still flowed in his veins, and he had not lost the outstanding political acumen of his Irish kinsmen. Adomnan tells us that, within

High Cross.

two years of his arrival on Iona, Columba had resolved to forge links with Brude, King of the Picts.

Having barely settled on Iona, Columba embarked on an even more ambitious and dangerous journey. He left the Christian coastal kingdom of Dalriada for the unknown lands of the pagan Picts.

For a man of faith like Columba, everything would take on a spiritual significance. His hazardous journey up the Great Glen in AD 565 would have reminded him of the epic journeys in the biblical texts he knew so well. He set out, like Abraham, not knowing what perils awaited him on the long road ahead.

His trek from Argyll to where Inverness lies today seems to have been an act of calculated – if risky – diplomacy. It was a show of spiritual muscle designed to impress the Picts, and to protect Iona's future. And, although the pagan Picts held Christianity in deep suspicion, it seems that, against all the odds, Columba earned the Picts' respect. He made an enormous impression on King Brude, who became convinced that the God that Columba worshipped was the omnipotent God and infinitely more powerful than the forces that he could deploy.

But, in the longer term, building bridges with hostile neighbours could be only one part of Columba's strategy for Iona's survival. More than anything, if he were going to make something of Iona, he would need the protection of military and political might. What Iona required was Dalriada's rulers to offer their protection to the Christian Church. And what better way to guarantee that protection than to arrange for Columba to choose those very rulers?

Conveniently for Columba, the High King of Irish Dalriada at that time happened to be a member of his own family. There is no doubt that Columba could shrewdly exploit his aristocratic connections to manipulate royal power for Iona's benefit. He decided to convince the political establishment that the Church should choose who the next king of Scottish Dalriada should be.

In a move of momentous historical significance, he anointed Aedan mac Gabrain as king. It was probably the earliest example of a churchman ordaining a king in Europe. Records show that it didn't happen elsewhere in Europe until the eighth century – probably as a result of monks from Iona travelling through the Continent.

Columba had become nothing less than a kingmaker. Through his aristocratic family ties and political skills, he had forged a radically new partnership between Church and State that would secure a future for Iona. Columba and the Church now had a close relationship with the King. They had a protector and sponsor who ranked among the most powerful people of their time.

Columba's role as kingmaker was of momentous historical significance.

Columba had never taken a narrow view. He had known from the very start that Iona's survival would depend upon his ability to engage with the world beyond Iona. He had now secured the support of Dalriada's political rulers and the tolerance of its enemies. And from the outside world also came all that Columba's monastery needed to thrive. In return for the skills and favour of Columba and his monks, Iona received the commodities it needed to flourish.

The monastery became a place of study and scholarship. It was also a centre for art and crafts. The monastery acted as church, school, hospital and trading post. It became a new and important part of the local economy. People would flock to the monastery on the feast day of a saint, and they would exchange stories and hold markets. It was a place of advice for kings and rulers, and a place to launch local initiatives. Many people came to Iona just to meet Columba. He consulted with rulers, and he sat in judgement on penitents, deciding on the most appropriate form of penance.

Iona Abbey today.

A significant part of the monks' time was devoted to the painstaking copying of sacred texts. Sixth-century Dalriada was a world in which basic literacy was revered – it was a highly marketable skill. Spiritual privileges, such as the promise of a burial on Iona, were much sought after by local kings, as Iona's religious reputation grew.

Columba's monastery began to develop emblematic architecture: the high crosses that still dominate the landscape. Unlike the later medieval buildings with church, cloister and tower that can be seen on Iona today, the monastery in Columba's time would have been little more of a cluster of huts. The central church would have been made of wood brought from the

Cloisters, Iona Abbey.

mainland, but the monks' huts or 'cells' would have been made from mud and wattle. Columba's own hut was positioned centrally. There was a common refectory and kitchen which also acted as a study and library. And on the west of the island was a guest house for pilgrims and other visitors. Unfortunately, very little remains today beyond the traces of postholes that indicate where buildings once stood.

As Iona built its reputation as a centre of learning and the arts, resources began to flow in. And the more it acquired, the more spectacular its achievements became. Among these were great illuminated works of literature, including, it is believed, the *Book of Kells*. For some of the manuscripts, around 200 calves had to be slaughtered to provide the skins necessary to produce the vellum. It was not long before these books began to convey something more than the text. They became the bearers of another message – about the wealth, power and status of the monasteries. They were to impress people.

High Cross, Iona.

The monastic order on Iona branched out, and new monasteries were founded on Tiree, at Loch Awe and on Skye. Each offered spiritual guidance and penance for lay people as well as for monks.

But of all Iona's satellite communities, perhaps the most significant – and also the most mysterious – was 'Hinba'. This elusive island was not only the sanctuary to which Columba himself retreated for periods of penance, but growing evidence suggests that it was also a substantial monastic settlement that acted as the spiritual power-house for Columba's monastic network. While Iona was the administrative and bureaucratic capital, Hinba was its spiritual heart.

Over the centuries, there have been many attempts to identify Hinba, but its location has always remained a mystery. People have tried to estimate how far away it was from Iona by using information about the time it took Columba to get there, but what is clear is that it was an out-of-the-way place. We know that it was a place where he could contemplate God in a deeper way than he could on Iona.

Now, a combination of ancient and twenty-first-century evidence has led some experts to suggest that this legendary cornerstone of Columba's monastic world was the island of Jura, the same waypoint that ensured Columba's safe passage from Ireland to Iona. Much of that evidence comes from references in the *Life of Columba* by Adomnan, but there are clues too in various place-names. The word 'Hinba' translates as 'the island with the great incision', which describes the shape of the island perfectly. On Jura, there is also a narrow corridor along Loch Tarbert, where there is a heavy concentration of church-related or religious place names. There were also sufficient natural resources on Jura at that time, such as deer, to support a monastic community. And last but not least, there was access to political centres of power.

With Hinba as its spiritual heart and Iona as its headquarters, the network of monasteries which Columba established gained huge reputation and wealth over time. Through his constant faith, political brilliance, and physical

Jura.

toughness, Columba created a northern strong-hold of Christianity virtually from scratch. His achievements in his thirty-four years in Scottish Dalriada were astonishing.

There is, however, still one piece missing from the puzzle. Although Columba's monasteries were dotted around Argyll, his influence barely dented vast swathes of the Highlands, not to mention the territories that lay beyond Gaeldom. Columba's diplomatic mission to the Picts might have been a good political move, but few Picts became Christians during Columba's lifetime. And without the conversion of the Picts who dominated the bulk of Scotland, there could be no meaningful spread of Christianity across the land. So how did Scotland become Christian?

Columba died in AD 597.

Adomnan makes it clear that Columba did not come to Scotland as a missionary. He came as an exile and a pilgrim undertaking penance. The stories never tell of him preaching the gospel in an attempt to convert people. Of course, once his network of monasteries had been established, even though the original intent had not been that of mission, they then provided a Christian influence in their location.

Nevertheless, when Columba died on Sunday, 9 June AD 597, most of Scotland was still pagan. And within 100 years of Columba's death, the influence of Iona had waned and the memory of its saintly founder was fading fast.

To solve the final mystery of how Columba earned his reputation as the man who brought Christianity to Scotland we must look to his biographer, Adomnan. His *Life of Columba*, written 100 years after Columba's death, is crucial to understanding the great paradox of Columba: how he became more powerful in death than in life.

Adomnan's Legacy

Adomnan, ninth Abbot of Iona, arrived on the scene at a difficult time. As it had struggled to expand its influence in the rest of Scotland, Iona had developed its own practices – practices that did not sit well with the seat of Christianity in distant Rome. Iona had one date for Easter, Rome another; Iona had translated some sacred texts into Gaelic – the language of the local

Iona.
Photograph: Joyce Watson

people – but Rome wanted everything to be in Latin. Iona's reluctance to conform was losing it prestige.

Adomnan longed to make Iona great again. He wanted to create a centre of excellence that would influence the whole of Christian Europe. And he decided he could best do this by writing a book.

It was a book that had got Columba into trouble in Ireland, and it would be a book that would make him a legend throughout Scotland. Adomnan's *Life of Columba* would inspire the monks of Iona with the memory of their powerful and mysterious founder.

Adomnan's great chronicle became not only a crucial source of evidence about Columba, it was also a very early example of written biography. In a sense, Adomnan was one of the first true historians and biographers. He was careful

to tell the reader the source of his evidence for the stories about Columba. This level of attention to detail, making careful efforts to prove that recounted events actually happened, was something new.

Nevertheless, Adomnan's book consists almost entirely of miracle stories. To the modern mind, such a book might seem of little historical value. But these were not simply fanciful tales. His *Life* was no less than a fantastically effective example of seventh-century spiritual 'spin'.

The founder of the Iona monastery was famous in Argyll. Tales of the great monk's saintly powers were exchanged in the fields and tracks of the countryside. Adomnan, however, set out to expand Columba's reputation. He transformed him from respected founding father of Iona to saintly embodiment of all that Iona – and Adomnan – stood for.

At first glance, the stories in Adomnan's *Life of Columba* appear to be a long list of examples of Columba's aptitude for prophecy, but patterns soon emerge. When Adomnan was constructing his figure of Columba, he was very much aware of the ways in which Columba's life paralleled the life of Christ. Many of Adomnan's stories tell of angels visiting Columba at decisive moments in his life. Other tales are of turning water into wine, or of healing the sick. Adomnan's stories are clearly designed to echo the life of Christ. They immediately plant in the reader's mind an idea: here is a saint in direct communion with Christ himself.

This is the first lesson that Adomnan expects us to learn from his chronicles: that Columba was an authentic saint.

The second type of story is the action and adventure kind. Columba's expedition to meet King Brude of the Picts is ideal material for *Boy's Own*

Life of Columba, by Adomnan.

tales. Adomnan tells us that when Columba reached Loch Ness, he came across a group of pagans who were in terror of a hideous beast that had risen from the dark waters of the loch. As Columba prepared to cross the water, the monster rose up to attack him and his followers. Undaunted, Columba raised his hand, made the sign of the cross and invoked the name of God. The Loch Ness monster fled. Columba defeated the beast by the power of the Almighty.

This is the second lesson that Adomnan expects us to learn from his chronicles: Columba is a match for anyone and anything. Nothing, neither the swords of men nor the storms of nature, can prevail against one who is filled with the strength of the all-powerful God.

Adomnan's stories tell of angels visiting Columba.

And this picture of Columba, as a formidable and wrathful spiritual warrior, was also created to champion a cause very close to Adomnan's heart: the setting up of laws which would guarantee the protection of the weak and defenceless.

In another story from the *Life of Columba*, Adomnan tells us of the time when Columba and a fellow monk were reading on the moors. A young girl appeared,

Adomnan's stories include action-adventures such as Columba's visit to Loch Ness and his encounter with the Loch Ness monster.

running to the monks for protection from a would-be attacker. Without pity for the girl or reverence for Columba, her pursuer speared her through Columba's cloak. Columba cursed the murderer to hell, and he fell, dead, on the spot.

This is a great story of divine rough justice – but there is more to it than that. In AD 697, Adomnan had proposed a radical, totally unprecedented piece of legislation. It was the first written code for the protection of non-combatants in armed conflict, and it specifically offered protection to those who were unable to protect themselves. It was no less than a prototype Geneva Convention. It was called the *Law of the Innocents*.

In effect, Adomnan's stories about Columba as champion of the defenceless leant weight to his own concerns about the impact of war and violence on the lives of women and children, and other non-combatants. The stories were part of a skilled publicity campaign in support of Adomnan's *Law of the Innocents*, which finally gained the approval of bishops and abbots from across both Irish and Scottish Dalriada.

However, this exercise would have been worth nothing if it had remained merely the wish list of a few holy men. Adomnan had to win the support of more than the Church. And so another key story that he tells us was intended to invoke Columba's authority in support of Adomnan's own most important project: his plan to ensure that Columba's greatest achievement in the political realm – the right to ordain kings – should survive. It was clear to Adomnan that the backing of kings was crucial if abbots wanted to continue to influence and regulate society for good.

This desire to influence politics is revealed in Adomnan's story of the angel that came to Columba to tell him to ordain Aedan mac Gabrain as King of Scottish Dalriada. At first, Columba defies the angel's wishes: Aedan is not the obvious heir to the throne. But the angel convinces Columba that Aedan is God's choice of king, and so Columba obliges, and Aedan is duly ordained.

Adomnan's message was clear: only God could choose kings, and the Church would make God's will known on Earth. In return for spiritual legitimacy, the crown would offer the Church its protection and support.

Adomnan was asserting the right of the Church to continue to be the royal power-broker. He knew that the backing of kings would enable the Law of the Innocents to be adopted throughout Dalriada. It would also secure the future of Scottish Christianity.

Adomnan's campaign was a resounding success. Through the development of a partnership between the political and spiritual spheres, standards of law and morality were woven into the fabric of Gaelic culture. And it gave the Church an unprecedented level of influence over wider society.

Jesus told his followers to render unto Caesar the things that are Caesar's and to God the things that are God's. The trouble is, 'How do you tell one from the other?' In time, the Church resolved this dilemma by claiming that since God was the source of all authority, including Caesar's, and since the Church was God's agent, it followed that the Church had final authority on earth. This is why the concept of Columba as kingmaker was of enormous symbolic importance. This claim of the Church to have final spiritual authority over

Columba's successors were kingmakers – and kingbreakers.

the State would resonate through the centuries from Columba's time to our own.

Not only were Columba and his successors portrayed as kingmakers; they were also shown to be king*breakers*. Kings were cursed and destroyed as a result of their wickedness or their failure to observe what Adomnan laid down as the proper way to behave.

But how did Columba and Adomnan's joint legacy spread from Iona to every corner of Scotland? By AD 716, Iona had fallen into line with Rome over the dating of Easter, and wars and conflict threatened to lessen its status. In the ninth century, Iona suffered terrible Viking invasions that would eventually leave it an empty shell. The island was overrun in AD 795 and it had its buildings burned again in AD 802. It is reported that no fewer than sixty-eight members of the monastic community were killed by the Norsemen in AD 806. Eventually, the monastery at Iona was abandoned and its monks dispersed, most of them returning to Ireland.

Columba's bones, however, were taken from Iona by the King of Scottish Dalriada, Kenneth MacAlpin. By the middle of the ninth century, he had pushed east into Pictland. Weakened by their own battles against the Vikings, the Picts quickly fell to MacAlpin, and the King was then able to bring together the territories of the Gaels and the Picts. In doing so, MacAlpin became the first king of the new Christian kingdom of Scotland, and his authority to rule over his Christian subjects was symbolised by Columba's bones – treasured relics representing the bond between Church and State.

Meanwhile, the legend of Columba went on. His name entered Viking mythology as a dark and wrathful presence, while Columba's crozier was held

Columba's treasured bones.

aloft as a talisman of victory-in-battle by the Scottish armies fighting against them. However, some Vikings settled in Argyll, became Christians themselves, and accepted Columba as their patron saint.

Columba was finally adopted as a symbol of Scotland's might and sovereignty. There can be no more powerful assertion of Columba's shaping influence on the politics of the nation state.

It is impossible to know whether Columba would have approved of all the causes that have invoked his name over the centuries. Unfortunately, saints have no control over the uses to which their images are put. In today's brand of 'Celtic Christianity', Columba is often seen as a gentle and welcoming figure, not the kind of person of whom we might be wary or afraid. But Columba, with his tremendous power was not someone whose company people would have found comfortable. And his legacy is just as challenging.

Iona.
Photograph: Joyce Watson

Two dominant themes emerged from the long gestation of Scottish Christianity. The first was the strong assertion by the Church of its spiritual authority over earthly politics. The second was its assertion of a certain independence in the way it interpreted the Christian tradition. These two themes were to prove a combustible mix in the centuries to come.

Columba and his successors transformed the Christian Church in Scotland from an eccentric outpost of a foreign religion into an equal partner in a new nation's political structure. Locked together in shaping the nation, Church and State would never cease to vie for ultimate dominance – and this struggle would set the scene for some of Scotland's most bitter and bloody conflicts.

PART 2
JOHN KNOX
THE GREAT BREAKING

John Knox.

On 19th August 1561, a small but determined delegation of Edinburgh worthies made its way to Holyrood Palace. Inside, the recently widowed Mary, Queen of Scots, was preparing to spend her first night in Scotland since returning from France as the nation's new monarch. Brought up at the French court, the nineteen-year-old Mary was both beautiful and highly educated. But she was also Catholic.

For John Knox, the leader of the delegation on that night, the presence of a Catholic Queen was intolerable, and the psalms that he and his companions had come to sing to Mary were not a welcome, but a warning.

The kings and rulers of the earth
Conspire and are all bent
Against the Lord, and Christ his son,
Whom he among us sent.

This is the image of John Knox that endures – the fiery, uncompromising preacher who challenged a queen. The problem, however, in common with other iconic figures from history, is that it is now very difficult to separate the man from the myth. Was Knox the heroic figure of Protestant legend who fearlessly challenged authority and single-handedly rescued Scotland from the clutches of Rome? Or was he the heretic who destroyed forever the unity of the one true Church as the sixteenth-century Catholic Church believed him to be? Or was he the misogynistic killjoy who pulled the plug on pleasure, as he is portrayed by modern myth?

The real man who emerges from behind the smokescreen of all these different perspectives is more complex, frail and fascinating than we might imagine.

Luther's Protestant ideas arrive in Scotland

John Knox did not set out to be a rebel with a cause. He followed a well-worn path for an educated young sixteenth-century man, and was ordained as a Catholic priest in the late 1530s.

This was, however, precisely the moment when the revolutionary Protestant thinking of Martin Luther was sweeping through Continental Europe. In order to understand the enormous significance of Luther's ideas, we have to keep in mind the momentous claim that Christianity made for itself: it offered men and women the possibility of eternal bliss or eternal damnation. The only issue was how heaven was to be achieved and hell avoided.

As Martin Luther agonised over how personal salvation and escape from hell was possible, he had an epiphany: we were not saved by prayers or pilgrimages, masses or indulgences, as the Church proclaimed. We were not even saved by our own good works. We were saved only by the grace of God. There was nothing in our humanity that justified us in the sight of God, only faith in his mercy. By the 1540s, these ideas were convulsing Europe and challenging the established order.

In 1527, Roman Catholic Scotland encountered Luther's Protestant ideas first-hand, when a young man named Patrick Hamilton preached in St

Martin Luther (1483–1546) (oil on canvas) by Lucas Cranach, the Elder (1472–1553).
Kurpfalzisches Museum, Heidelberg, Germany/Bridgeman Art Library.

Andrews, the town where John Knox was educated. Hamilton had studied theology in Paris, where he had been gripped by the new ideas. However, in Scotland, Hamilton was swiftly branded a heretic by the Church, and executed. His martyrdom outside St Salvator's College in St Andrews is still commemorated every year by students in the town. The spot on which he was burned at the stake – taking six hours to die in a horribly botched execution – is marked by his initials laid in cobblestones.

The spot at which Patrick Hamilton was burned at the stake.

But if the Roman Catholic Church believed that Hamilton's execution would put an end to the preaching of Protestant heresy, they could not have been more wrong. St Andrews was buzzing with talk about these new ideas, and his death sent shock waves around Scotland. It was said that the 'reek of Mr Hamilton infected all it blew upon' – with the notable exception, it would seem, of John Knox.

After his ordination as a priest, Knox took up work as a notary and, later, as a tutor. He showed no particular interest in the new Protestant ideas, and he seems to have worked contentedly within the Church until the preacher, George Wishart, came to Scotland.

George Wishart was, himself, an unlikely revolutionary. He was gentle and serious and, while still a student at Cambridge, he regularly gave food and clothing to the poor. It was said that he even donated the sheet from his bed every time he changed it. But Wishart had come to believe that the Roman Catholic Church had lost its way, and he was not afraid to make his views known.

In sixteenth-century Scotland, it was dangerous enough to believe in anything that might be interpreted as heretical, but it was downright suicidal to try to persuade other people to believe it with you. It must, therefore, have taken enormous courage for George Wishart to have agreed to an extensive preaching tour of Scotland in 1544. His tour was not authorised by any part of the establishment, and there was no doubt that, in the eyes of the Church, he was spreading a dangerous, heretical message.

When he heard Wishart preach, Knox was electrified. Here was a young man, almost exactly the same age as himself, speaking directly and passionately about a personal relationship with God – and risking everything to do so. Fired with the excitement of his new-found convictions, Knox threw in his lot with Wishart and, sometime around January 1546, joined him in his itinerant preaching. He acted as a bodyguard for Wishart, carrying a double-handed sword – the claymore – for protection. Knox was clearly proud to help.

The claymore.

They caused quite a stir wherever they went, and so it was only a matter of time before they came to the attention of the Catholic Archbishop of St Andrews, Cardinal David Beaton. He was a career churchman, a statesman and the Primate of Scotland.

St Andrews was the ecclesiastical capital of Scotland and a tourist hot spot then as now. Thousands of people poured into the town every year to worship at the shrine of Scotland's patron saint, and this medieval tourist trade had helped to make Cardinal Beaton richer even than the monarch.

Despite the intimations coming from the Continent, Beaton had little interest in Church reform, and he saw Wishart and Knox simply as heretics defying the authority of the Church. They would have to be dealt with.

St Andrews.

St Andrews Castle.
Photograph: David Quinn

While preaching in East Lothian, Wishart was warned that his arrest was imminent. He sent Knox away to safety, telling him: 'One person is sufficient for a sacrifice'. Knox's two-handed sword was never put to use. Wishart was arrested and incarcerated within the dungeon of St Andrews Castle. He was tried and duly sentenced to death. When invited by the Church to make a last confession, he gave no sign of recanting.

On 1st March 1546, Wishart was brought under guard from his cell in the sea-tower to the forecourt of St Andrews Castle. The executioners stuffed his pockets with gunpowder before he was tied to a stake and set alight. Some said that the gunpowder was to create a fireworks display for Cardinal Beaton to enjoy as he watched from the window of his private apartment. But the truth is more banal. The executioners lacked practice at burning

heretics, and the gunpowder was added to make sure that Wishart would burn quickly.

As well as enormous courage, it takes a faith that is deeply rooted to motivate a person to die for an idea. Wishart's martyrdom proved how important the Protestant faith had become – now far too deep for even a cardinal to uproot.

Wishart's martyrdom made a huge impact upon Knox, but his immediate concern was to evade capture, and he went into hiding. He even considered fleeing abroad. In the meantime, however, some more militant Protestants had decided on revenge.

Early on the morning of 29th May, just three months after Wishart's execution, a small band of Protestant sympathisers gained entry to St Andrews Castle. It was not difficult for them to slip in while the drawbridge was lowered to let workmen in. By the time the porter realised what was happening, it was too late. The conspirators surprised Cardinal Beaton in his bedchamber and, ignoring his pleas not to kill him because he was a priest, they stabbed him to death.

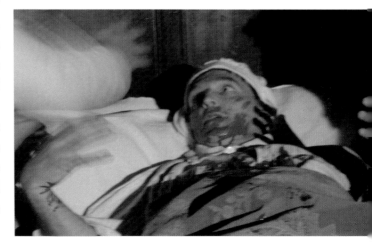

As soon as word got out, people from the town came running to find out what was happening. To prove that the Cardinal was dead, the perpetrators hung Beaton's mutilated corpse from the very window from which he had watched Wishart burn.

The conspirators decided to occupy the castle, which was well fortified and seemed to be impregnable. And soon this small gang of conspirators found themselves at the centre of a growing camp of Protestant rebels. They may have been surprised by the number of people who flocked to the castle, perhaps now seeing it as a symbol of defiance. The actions of the conspirators had struck a blow for Protestantism, right at the heart of the Catholic regime.

The Castle at St Andrews.

The government, however, was quick to react, and the castle was besieged by troops. The siege that followed was typical of the sixteenth-century Scottish habit of both talking to the enemy and fighting at the same time. Despite being officially under siege, there was constant negotiation, with people coming in and out of the castle quite freely.

As time passed, the castle became a focus for religious debate. The first congregation of the Protestant Church was formed within its walls. Gradually, its occupants were joined by other dissidents and malcontents. Among those choosing to join this community was John Knox.

As the siege continued outside, Knox resumed his duties as a tutor, and set about teaching his pupils the new Protestant beliefs. While lecturing on a passage from St John's Gospel, he was overheard by the castle's resident preacher. Deeply impressed by Knox's skills as a communicator, the preacher immediately tried to sign him up as an apologist for the Protestant cause. Knox refused point blank. He said that he would not run where God had not called him. Perhaps he just did not feel cut out to be a preacher. Or maybe he had no desire to raise his head above the parapet quite so soon after his recent brush with danger as an associate of Wishart.

But the castle preacher was unwilling to accept 'no' for an answer and, during the course of a sermon, he put Knox on the spot by calling him again in public. In front of everyone, Knox was so overcome that, as he later described it himself, he 'burst forth in most abundant tears and withdrew ... to his chamber'. It was clear that Knox did not feel called to become a preacher.

That might well have been the end of the matter. We might never have heard of John Knox at all, had it not been for another John: John Winram. He was to have a profound impact both on the life of Knox and on the progress of the Reformation in Scotland.

As a leading churchman, Winram had taken charge in St Andrews following Beaton's murder, until a new archbishop could be appointed. Unlike Beaton, however, Winram was already convinced of the need for reform. To try to encourage debate on the issue, he agreed to a series of sermons in the parish church. It was in this context that Knox first preached.

The Castle at St Andrews was under siege.

Whether the pressure from his peers finally proved irresistible, or whether he came to believe finally that God had called him, Knox eventually took to the pulpit. His sermon was preached in Holy Trinity Church, St Andrews. It was the first time that the wrathful incantatory voice that was to change the history of Scotland was heard.

Knox preached from the Book of Revelation, and this first sermon was very characteristic of him, full of fire and thunder, drawing on apocalyptic imagery, and denouncing the Roman Catholic Church as the Antichrist. This

Stained-glass window at Holy Trinity Church, St Andrews.

is the mature voice of Knox – anti-Catholic, going straight for the heart of the matter and full of violent language and vehemence.

But this sort of language must have seemed entirely appropriate to him. The sixteenth century was a period of great upheaval, both in Scotland and on the Continent. With wars and religious persecution tearing Europe apart, it must have seemed to many people that the end of the world was truly nigh. Knox certainly seems to have interpreted his age in this way.

It probably accounts for the increasing ferocity of his language. Judgement was coming upon the world, and people had to take sides. There could be *no* compromise. Either you were for God and the Protestant cause, or you were on the side of the Devil. Knox was not a man interested in shades of grey.

Today, we might like to think of ourselves as quite distant from these sorts of views, but this kind of approach is not uncommon – even in the twenty-first century. Islamic fundamentalists and the western politicians who oppose them often talk, in apocalyptic terms, of light versus darkness and good versus evil, and there is no compromise in their world-view.

Of course, in his spiritual battle, Knox was convinced that he was on the side of the angels. The dangers and difficulties that he had faced in the eighteen months since he had embraced the Protestant cause only made him more certain that he was right. He believed that he had found his vocation as a Protestant preacher and, given the encouraging developments in St Andrews, it must have seemed to him as if reform of the whole Scottish Church was just around the corner.

Then, however, the French fleet sailed into St Andrews bay, and all his hopes were dashed.

Knox leaves Scotland

Although St Andrews Castle was in the hands of the reformers, Scotland in 1547 was still very much a Catholic country. The widowed Scottish Queen, the French-born Mary of Guise, had called on her countrymen to help her regain control of the castle and rid her of these troublesome Protestants.

When Mary had married the Scottish king, James V, an alliance had been cemented between Catholic France and Catholic Scotland, symbolised by the birth of their daughter Mary, the future Queen of Scots. But the young Mary's eventual accession was now under threat from the growing momentum of the Protestant rebellion.

The French fleet swiftly bombarded the castle into submission, over-whelming the Protestant rebels. With the uprising crushed, it was time to deal with the perpetrators. Those in the castle had bonded together as fellow revolutionaries, regardless of their background. Now, however, the French separated the nobles and other high-ranking men from the rest. The former were treated almost like guests, while the latter, including Knox, were sent to work on galley ships.

Nothing in Knox's life had prepared him for this experience. French galley ships of this time were about 100–150 feet long and about thirty feet wide. They were equipped with sails but, when the winds died, they relied on the rowers – six men fettered to each oar who ate, slept and relieved themselves where they sat.

Under the watchful eye of his French Catholic guards, Knox could only seethe in silence and try not to give in to utter despair. Now, the firebrand preacher was reduced to sly and solitary acts of defiance. He later tells, for example, of the occasion on which he was given an image of the Blessed Virgin Mary to kiss. Not being prepared to do this, he threw the icon overboard – but not without checking first that no-one was watching.

This seems typical of him. Although Knox was prepared to defy authority, he clearly had no appetite for physical danger, and certainly had no martyr complex. He was never reckless enough to put himself deliberately in the way of pain or death. Nevertheless, while aboard the French galley his spirit was not broken by failure and hardship. At times, it looked to him as though Satan had won; but, through these darkest days, Knox believed that Satan would eventually be defeated.

In February 1549, Knox was finally freed from the galleys after nineteen punishing months. While he had been away, Scotland had been heavily reinforced by the French. So, although he was now free to return to Scotland, Knox was unwilling to risk returning and, like many Scottish reformers before him, sought sanctuary in England – in the border town of Berwick-upon-Tweed.

Berwick-upon-Tweed.

England had become a refuge for reformers from all across Europe. The Reformation in England was flourishing under the young King Edward VI. Sandwiched between the two Catholic powers of Scotland and France, Edward's England was a thorn in both their sides.

Knox had learned a hard lesson from the events in St Andrews Castle. It must have seemed to him now that joining the rebels, confident of their ultimate victory, had been a grave miscalculation for which he'd had to pay a heavy price. He did not intend to make the same mistake again. From now on, Knox would be cautious. He would go only where he was welcome. And in Berwick he was made to feel very welcome.

As a charismatic preacher, the thirty-five-year-old Knox soon attracted around him a coterie of devoted followers – many of them women. In an age when most marriages were arranged, it was quite common for women to form close emotional relationships with their parish priest, rather than with a husband who saw their marriage purely as a contractual arrangement. As the Reformation gained ground, it was natural for them to do the same with Protestant ministers like Knox.

Shortly after his arrival in Berwick, Knox was introduced to Elizabeth Bowes, the wife of the English captain at Norham Castle. It was to be the beginning of an intimate, life-long relationship.

Although Elizabeth was not much older than Knox, she had already borne her husband fifteen children. She seems to have become a Protestant before Knox arrived in Berwick; but, throughout her life, she struggled with doubts. It was to Knox that she turned for reassurance and support. And Knox, who was so fierce and unyielding in his public pronouncements, was always gentle and understanding in his dealings with Elizabeth.

While women were generally regarded at this time as inferior to men, and as temptresses of men, within the medieval church they had a status. So Knox took Elizabeth's spiritual torments seriously, and dealt with her sensitively.

But, from the beginning, there were accusations of sexual impropriety. It was the intensity of their relationship that set the tongues wagging. Elizabeth was deeply emotionally dependent on Knox, but he was just as committed to her. Knox wrote: 'I have always delighted in your company and, when labours would permit, you know I would spend hours talking and communing with you . . .'.

Was there a sexual subtext to their relationship? There is often a fine line between pastoral care and passionate love, and Knox confessed: 'In my body you think I am no adulterer – let that be, but the heart is infected with foul lusts. Externally, I commit no adultery, but my wicked heart loveth the self, and cannot refrain from vain imaginations.'

Knox and Elizabeth remained close until her death.

Nevertheless, their affection and need for each other was controlled by their sincere religious convictions. But Knox's marriage to Elizabeth's daughter, Marjory, would ensure that they would always be close.

As a poor preacher, Knox could have had no hope of proposing to Marjory; and her father, Captain Bowes, was totally opposed to the match. Nevertheless, Knox and Marjory were betrothed, and Elizabeth remained an intimate part of Knox's life until the day she died – even if it was as his mother-in-law.

England took Knox to her heart.

Meanwhile, England had also taken Knox to her heart.

The Reformation in England had the full backing of King Edward VI and his advisors, and Knox's impressive and fiery preaching skills were soon noticed at court. He was invited to become one of the royal chaplains in 1551, and Knox accepted the post. He could have been forgiven for feeling quite satisfied with his life. He had found acceptance in England, and he had the ear of the King; he was surrounded by devoted followers and adoring women; he was engaged to be married and he was financially secure.

But he was far from happy. He felt that change was being introduced too slowly, and that the Edwardian Church was being compromised by some less-than-godly royal advisors. Knox believed that the English Reformation had not gone far enough.

Mary Tudor (Hans Eworth, 1540–1573).
Courtesy of the National Portrait Gallery, London.

He was filled with a terrible sense of foreboding. He wrote:

> If you, O England, for any respect delay your repentance and conversion unto God; if you shall retain in honour and authority such as have declared themselves enemies of God, then I and others who faithfully have warned you of your duty and of vengeance to come, shall be clean of your blood.

Knox came to believe that it was only a matter of time before God wreaked his vengeance on faithless England. And sure enough, in July 1553, the King died.

Overnight, everything changed. Edward, the great Protestant hope, was succeeded by his half-sister, Mary Tudor. Unlike her brother, however, Mary was a committed Catholic.

Upon her accession, Mary unleashed a campaign of terror, in her mission to restore England to Roman Catholicism. The new Queen was to become known as 'Bloody Mary' – and for good reason. She set about expunging all evidence of Protestantism. Protestant literature was destroyed, and preachers were burned as heretics.

To Knox, it looked like the end of the world. These were terrible times for Protestants in England, and Knox decided to do what he usually did in these situations: he got out.

As Protestants burned, Knox fled to the Continent, leaving behind the people who had shown him such kindness. From his letters, we do know that

Knox wrote to his English friends from the safety of Geneva.

he felt uneasy about abandoning his beloved English sisters and brothers to their fate:

> If I thought that I might have your presence, I would jeopardise my own life to let men see what may be done with a safe conscience in these dangerous days . . . But seeing that it cannot be done instantly, without danger to others than to me, I will abide the time that God shall appoint.

We can hear his embarrassment in his letters. He was well aware that he was encouraging others to stay and face the terrors of Mary's England, while he was writing from the safety of the Continent.

And although he was telling his friends to remain in England, he arranged for his wife and his mother-in-law to join him. Together, they made their way to what was to become Knox's true spiritual home – the centre of radical Protestantism, the Swiss city of Geneva.

Geneva.

Geneva's internationalism was as strong then as it is today. In the sixteenth century, it was the centre of a radical social and theological experiment, presided over by John Calvin. Protestants from all over Europe flocked to the city to be part of it.

Martin Luther, the monk, may have agonised over whether he would be saved from the wrath of God, but John Calvin, the lawyer, confidently reckoned that it was possible to prove whom God had already chosen to join Him in

Portrait of John Calvin (1509–1564) (oil on canvas) by Titian (Tiziano Vecellio) (c.1488–1576).
The Reformed Church of France, Paris, France/Bridgeman Art Library.

Geneva's ancient cathedral: stark and simple.

the afterlife. Once the faithful had that assurance of salvation, they could stop agonising over their eternal destiny and get on with the job of creating a true reflection of Heaven on earth.

And, under Calvin, the new city of God was established here on earth in the form of Geneva. The ancient Cathedral, once vivid with its altars and images, was stripped bare of anything that might distract the soul from its pure encounter with God. It was a place of utter starkness and simplicity. Knox loved it. The bareness of the church was an indication of the reformers' deep-rooted fear of idolatory – the idea that anything humanly created could represent God. They seemed to miss the fact that theology itself was humanly created, and that a conceptual idol might be as dangerous as a physical one.

Unlike the imperfect Protestant state he had experienced in England, Knox believed that Geneva was a city where the State had been brought uncompromisingly into line with the Protestant religion. It was perfect. He claimed that Geneva was the most godly place on earth since the days of the apostles.

As in England, Knox's charismatic preaching skills soon drew another loyal circle of female supporters around him. They included not only his wife and mother-in-law but also women friends who had joined him from England. These were women who had been suffering under the rule of Bloody Mary, and who were longing for his company. To one friend in London, Anna Locke, he wrote:

> You write that your desire is earnest to see me. Dear Sister, if I could express the thirst and languor I have had for your presence, I should

appear to pass measure. Yea I weep and rejoice in remembrance of you, but that would vanish by the comfort of your presence, which I assure you is so dear to me that if the charge of this little flock did not impede me, I should be with you before this letter could reach you . . .

It is clear that the period during which he lived in Geneva was the happiest time of Knox's life. He was now married, his two sons were born there and he had the comfort of a congregation that he felt was entirely committed to the cause. They provided him with the sense of being part of a godly community. The total commitment of the whole congregation, all of whom had come into exile for their faith, was, for Knox, the ideal.

Protestantism rises in Scotland

Unfortunately, this happiness was not to last. In March 1557, a group of reform-minded nobles invited Knox to come back to Scotland. Known as the Lords of the Congregation, they had signed a common bond, the first of many covenants which bound them to work together against the Catholic State for the establishment of a reformed Kirk.

This was a very significant moment in the Reformation, because it was the first public affirmation of noble support. The nobles were quite clearly stating that they were prepared to support their convictions with military muscle.

Even with this overt support for the Protestant cause in Scotland, Knox had no intention of leaving either Calvin's heaven-on-earth, or his own coterie. It took Calvin himself to remind Knox that the reason he was in Geneva in the first place was to observe the great Protestant experiment, and to export it to Scotland. Knox left his beloved Geneva reluctantly. What he did not know was that he would be walking into history.

His journey back to Scotland was not easy. When he reached Dieppe on the French coast, Knox suddenly received word again from the Lords of the Congregation – he was now to hold fire and wait on the Continent.

Knox was furious: 'To some it may appear a small matter that I have abandoned my public office, leaving my poor family destitute and my beloved flock to the charge of another. But to me it is no small matter.'

He accused the nobles of allowing politics to dictate their actions, rather than the Word of God. It was an unfair charge that revealed more about his own ambiguity about returning to Scotland than about the motives of the Lords of the Congregation.

Stuck unexpectedly in Dieppe, in a foul mood, and hearing more stories by the day of the terrible sufferings of his brothers and sisters under the rule of the English Queen, Bloody Mary, Knox sat down to compose a text denouncing her tyrannical rule – *The First Blast of the Trumpet against the Monstrous Regiment of Women*.

The first sentence of Knox's *Blast* leaves us in no doubt as to the purpose of his treatise:

> To promote a woman to bear rule, superiority, dominion, or empire above any realm, nation, or city, is repugnant to nature, contumely to God, a thing most contrarious to his revealed will and approved ordinance, and finally it is the subversion of good order, of all equity and justice.

This was, of course, an attack upon the *rule* of women and not against women as such. Mary, the Catholic queen, was reigning in England at the time that he was writing, and was clearly the prime target of Knox's invective. But Mary died in November 1558, and was immediately succeeded by her half-sister, Elizabeth. Queen Elizabeth I of England was the great hope of all English Protestants – as indeed she was of Knox himself.

Knox's timing was disastrous. He had just written a book arguing that no woman should rule. He could hardly add an addendum, 'I didn't mean you, ma'am.' Elizabeth was incandescent with rage.

And Elizabeth was not the only one who was furious. Knox's great hero and mentor, Calvin, described *The First Blast* as a piece of 'thoughtless arrogance'. But, at the time of writing, Knox had felt that he had no choice. As ever, there could be no compromise. He had to preach God's word, no matter how it was received. Knox saw himself as an Old Testament prophet, sent to bring the news no-one wanted to hear.

Now, though, there was no prospect of his ever returning to England. For Knox, there was only one place to go: Scotland.

In his absence, the Reformation had secretly been making slow and deliberate progress. The Protestant nobles had organised to plot both the removal of the Catholic French and the Regent, Mary of Guise.

In St Andrews, John Winram, the man who had first given Knox the opportunity to find his voice as a preacher, had used the intervening years well. He had remained within the Catholic Church, but he had stacked his priory with reform-minded priests who would provide the manpower for the new Protestant Church when it emerged.

When, on St Giles' day, rioters broke up a Catholic procession in Edinburgh, it was a sign that a Protestant revolution was gaining momentum among ordinary people.

The Queen Regent in Scotland saw that the situation was getting out of control. She had to act, and passed a decree in 1559 outlawing leading Protestant preachers. The final battle was approaching, and it was at this critical moment that the prodigal son, John Knox, returned.

As soon as Knox landed, he was thrust into the very heart of things. His gifts as a charismatic preacher meant that he could be used to trigger events. Whether he knew it or not, he was being used as a 'rabble-rouser'.

Knox was sent by the Protestant nobles to preach at the Church of St John in Perth in May 1559. Perth was no random choice. The town was already a tinderbox – riven by class tensions, and on the brink of erupting into violence.

The response of the congregation to Knox's sermon was to tear down the statues and the altars and all the signs and symbols of Catholic spirituality. His sermon was a battle cry for armed confrontation with the forces of the Regent, Mary of Guise, who, once again, called on the French to help her deal with the Protestant threat.

Knox finally found the courage to throw himself into the fray. As chaplain and morale-booster, with the odds stacked against them, he marched with the Protestant troops. Within a short period of time, they had seized control of St Andrews. The ecclesiastical capital of Scotland had fallen.

This was the tipping point. This was the moment when 'The Great Breaking' finally happened. Later, in the autumn of that year, Knox was appointed Protestant minister of St Andrews, twelve years after he had preached his first historic sermon there.

The reform-minded priests whom John Winram had attracted to his priory in St Andrews were now ready to go out into the parishes and take their places as the first generation of Protestant ministers.

Winram was joined by significant numbers of previously Catholic clergy. Many of them were well-educated: Augustinians, Dominicans and Franciscans. Of course, it is also worth noting that these men were now faced with the choice of joining the Protestant Church or facing unemployment. Unsurprisingly, many were able to see a place for themselves within Protestantism.

Military conflict continued but, by June 1560, the French army had been driven back to Leith and placed under siege. Then, quite unexpectedly, it was all over.

Mary of Guise died at Edinburgh Castle. With this event, the whole political landscape changed. A treaty was signed between the Scots and the French. In return for a Protestant parliament, the Scottish nobles agreed that the Regent's daughter could take up her throne. But the conditions were clear: although Mary, now Queen of Scots, was a Catholic, she would only be allowed to govern as the monarch of a Protestant people.

Edinburgh.

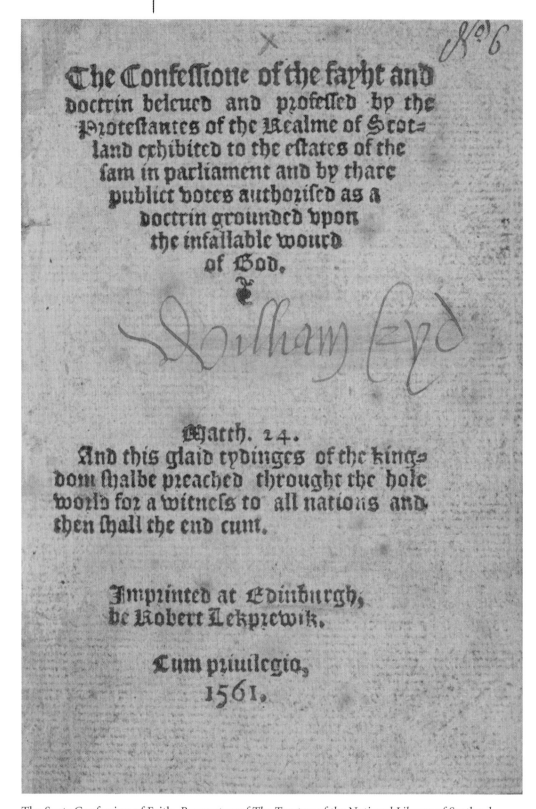

The Scots Confession of Faith. *By courtesy of The Trustees of the National Library of Scotland.*

The important point about the summer of 1560 was that all of this was made not just public but official. Parliament made Protestantism the official religion of the realm. It abolished the Mass and the other sacraments.

It did positive things too. It adopted *The Scots Confession of Faith*, which laid down very precisely what Protestants believed. This document was drawn up by Knox, John Winram and four other ministers, outlining in clear, unambiguous language the key doctrines of the Protestant faith. [See Appendix for the text of *The Scots Confession*.]

All of this made it absolutely plain to the rest of Europe that Scotland had finally adopted Protestantism.

At last, Knox had achieved his goal. This was his moment of triumph. He was appointed minister of St Giles' in Edinburgh, the capital city. The exile was once again at the very heart of things.

However, after the revolution comes the long process of bedding in – of making revolutionary ideas and insights work in the real lives of human beings – and that is a messy business. More shades of grey than black and white. It soon became clear that this was not a job to which Knox was suited temperamentally. In his theology, there was only good or evil. And in his life, there was no room for compromise. Other religious leaders, like John Winram, who had lived in Scotland all their lives and knew the Scottish people and the politics of the Scottish church, were better equipped to deal with these nuances. Without the abrasive certainty of Knox, Winram seems to have been able to carry people with him through the process of Reformation. Knox, on the other hand, found himself gradually being eased out.

He began to despair. This was not the perfect Protestant revolution Knox had anticipated. And worse was to follow: in November, his wife, Marjory, died. Knox was devastated.

Knox – Architect of the Reformation?

From Knox's point of view, the political situation was also becoming intolerable. Mary, Queen of Scots, had returned from France in August 1561 to take up her throne. Knox was immediately anxious that she would attempt to reintroduce Catholicism. He had good reason to fear – while living on the Continent, he had heard first-hand how Mary's uncles had persecuted French Protestants. Knox was adamant: there must be no compromise with this new Catholic Queen.

So when Knox heard that the nobles had agreed that Mary could continue to hear Mass in her private chapel, he was furious. He railed that the courtiers had 'departed from the purity of God's word, that they had begun to follow the ways of the world, and so, again, to shake hands with the Devil and with idolatry'.

To Knox, it looked as though what had happened in England was about to happen all over again in Scotland. God would judge the Scots, as he had judged the English for their faithlessness, with a terrible persecution at the hands of a Catholic Queen.

And Knox's fears were exacerbated by the fact that Edinburgh was still largely Catholic in its sympathies. It was he, and not Mary, who was in a hostile environment. His task was the toughest job in Scotland: to convert Edinburgh to Protestantism.

So, vulnerable and isolated, Knox led his delegation of concerned Protestant citizens to Holyrood Palace to sing psalms outside Mary's window. What, at first sight, might have looked like an act of triumphalism was, in fact, an act of desperation. Their ragged voices sang:

> The kings and rulers of the earth
> Conspire and are all bent
> Against the Lord, and Christ his son,
> Whom he among us sent.

To the Protestant nobles, Knox was rapidly becoming an embarrassment. They had agreed to the Queen's return as the price to be paid for a Protestant State – but, for Knox, that price was too high.

In the meantime, Mary decided to take the initiative. In an effort to win Knox over, the young Queen summoned him to a series of meetings to discuss his violent and vocal opposition to her. She even offered him a post as a kind of Royal Chaplain. If he did not want to accept that post, she, at least, hoped that he would explain his views to her.

But Knox was wary and distrustful, and chose not to take up her offer. Perhaps he was afraid of being won over by her personal charm, or of being sucked into court politics. Or, perhaps, once more, the fear of compromising his Protestant beliefs led Knox to refuse. The meetings were a disaster, further distancing Knox from his lawful Queen. He was now more fearful than ever, but he could not persuade the nobles in Scotland to listen to him.

In desperation, Knox even briefly considered summoning the godly to arms:

Mary, Queen of Scots (1542–1587) and John Knox (c.1512–1572) by Samuel Sidley (1829–1896). Towneley Hall Art Gallery and Museum, Burnley, Lancashire/Bridgeman Art Library.

If you think that I or any other preacher within this realm may amend such enormities, you are deceived. For we have discharged our consciences, but remedy there appeareth none, unless we would arm the hands of the people in whom abideth yet some spark of God's fear.

When Mary chose the young Catholic nobleman, Lord Darnley, as her husband, Knox became even more paranoid. What better evidence was there of a papist plot to reverse the hard-won achievements of the Reformation? His prophecies of doom seemed to be coming true. But what could he do about it?

When Darnley attended the service at St Giles' on his first Sunday as Mary's husband, it was probably as a gesture of goodwill. Knox, however, used the opportunity to preach a sermon based on the Old Testament story of King Ahab and his wicked Queen, Jezebel:

Statue of John Knox in St Giles'.

Ahab received many great benefits of God. And how did Ahab thank God for his great benefit received? Did he remove his idolatry? Did he correct his idolatrous wife, Jezebel? No, we find no such thing; for the last visitation of God was, that dogs licked the blood of one, and did eat the flesh of the other.

It was obvious to everyone that he meant to equate the royal couple with Ahab and Jezebel. This time, he had gone too far. Restrictions were placed upon where and when Knox could preach in future.

The truth is that, as Protestantism was becoming respectable, Knox was becoming more and more of an embarrassment and his outbursts were becoming ever more scandalous.

Then, rumours of a French and Spanish crusade against Protestants began to circulate. Convinced that a Catholic conspiracy was going to overthrow the fledgling Protestant State – but unable to persuade the Protestant nobles to take action – Knox, as he had done on so many occasions before, decided to remove himself from the line of fire.

Knox withdrew from public life, and turned his attention to private matters. In 1564, he had remarried at the age of fifty. His bride, Margaret Stewart, was just sixteen years old. Over the next six years, they had three daughters. But even then, his relationship with his former mother-in-law, Elizabeth Bowes, continued to cause comment.

Knox was still dogged by accusations of sexual impropriety – and, after Elizabeth died in 1572, he felt compelled to publish a refutation of the charges:

'I . . . declare to the world what was the cause of our great familiarity and long acquaintance; which was neither flesh nor blood, but a troubled conscience upon her part'.

In his remaining years, unable to make any real impact upon public affairs, Knox was reduced to railing from the pulpit. In the end, his voice was too weak to carry in the great Church of St Giles, and he had to preach in its smaller Tollbooth section instead.

Knox preached his last sermon on 9th November 1572 at the induction of his chosen successor. He had believed for some time that he was dying, and, in his letters, he seemed ready, almost eager to go: 'I heartily salute and take goodnight of the faithful in both the realms . . . for as the world is weary of me, so am I of it'.

The last two weeks of his life were spent privately at his home in Edinburgh with his young wife, and daughters aged seven, six and just two. Towards the end, Knox asked his wife to read to him from the Gospel of John, Chapter 17, the place, he said, where he had cast his 'first anchor': 'I have shown your glory on earth; I have finished the work you gave me to do. Give me glory in your presence now.'

John Knox died on 24th November 1572, aged fifty-nine. He is buried at an unmarked spot outside St Giles' Cathedral in Edinburgh.

At Knox's funeral, the Earl of Morton described him as a man who never feared – but the irony is that his last writings were filled with fear and foreboding.

He did not know that the Reformation was secure and that the Protestant Kirk in Scotland would triumph and be the dominant church in the following centuries. He was depressed, weary and ill – and, as he looked around him, what he saw were the things that might go wrong and the things that were not working, rather than the things that were.

John Winram, the canny politician, on the other hand, lived to see the Reformation take root and flourish. From his base in St Andrews, he oversaw his Protestant ministers as they slowly but surely imprinted the new religion on Scotland, and the Reformation programme, with its emphasis on a godly, educated society, was rolled out across the nation. There would be a huge increase in the provision of schools, and, through the work of the new Kirk Sessions, a concern for poor relief and moral discipline. The Protestant

The Scottish flag.

Reformation, which Knox had believed to be a failure, would be permanently secured.

And after Knox's death, Mary's own tragic story would unfold. She would lose the support of the nobles and, ultimately, her life at the hands of her English cousin, Elizabeth I.

So, in the end, what can we say about the man behind all the myths?

Dour woman-hater? Far from it. He was married twice, and a father to five children. He enjoyed close and genuinely loving relationships with women throughout his life. In fact, it is doubtful whether he could have carried on with his work without the emotional and psychological support of his network of women friends and supporters.

Architect of the Scottish Reformation? Hardly. Knox did not even live in Scotland for most of the decade leading up to 1560. His voice was important, and it may have been the loudest when the final moment of revolution came; but it was one voice among many. As we have seen, others like John Winram had prepared for and soon took over the practical task of implementing the Protestant revolution.

Brave warrior for truth? Some will admire the man who will not compromise – who clings to Truth with a capital 'T'. But others will admire even more the people Knox so despised – the ones who were prepared to take risks in order to find a way of living with people different from themselves. For if the struggles of the sixteenth-century Scottish Church teach us anything, it is that no human being, or system, or Church, can ever contain the whole truth about anything.

PART 3
COVENANTERS
THE KILLING TIMES

In 1684, Lowland Scotland was under occupation by government-sanctioned militias. Their task was to hunt down those who refused to surrender their religious beliefs. This period came to be known as the 'Killing Times', and the men and women who were being persecuted were the last of the Covenanters. In Part 3, we discover who the Covenanters were, and what exactly they believed that was so subversive that the State wanted them dead.

The Rise of the Covenanters

It is hard to imagine now, looking at the average Church of Scotland congregation, that there was once a time when they were 'Scotland's Most Wanted'. But they were.

The Killing Times marked the end of a long downward spiral for Scotland's youngest Christian movement – Presbyterianism. Since the start of the Protestant Reformation in the middle of the sixteenth century, Presbyterians had fought for the freedom to worship as they chose, and they had rejected control of the Church by bishops and monarchs. Now they were faced with a dreadful choice: submit to the authority of the King, or resist. And those who resisted would pay with their lives.

But how did things get so bad for Presbyterians? After all, the Scottish Reformation had, apparently, left them in the ascendancy.

The Reformation in Scotland had been an attempt to revitalise Christianity at the grass roots. Many people had felt that the Catholic Church had forgotten about the impoverished parishes, while the highest levels of the Church became fabulously wealthy. The work of firebrand preachers like John Knox had set the Reformation alight, but disillusionment with the Catholic Church at parish

level had fanned the flames. In this fire was forged the new Protestant move-ment of Presbyterianism.

Presbyterianism placed a new emphasis on 'the people'. There would be no bishops and no hierarchy in the Kirk. We should remember, however, that the Reformation did not happen overnight. This young Christian movement still had to face a formidable fight for survival.

In terms of religious allegiance, Scotland was a messy patchwork: huge swathes of the land, especially in the Highlands, were fervently Catholic. Even in the Presbyterian heartland, the Lowlands, many people still clung to the familiar rituals and festivals of the old order. Convincing them of the rightness of the new religion was going to be an uphill struggle.

But the greatest obstacle to the new church was the monarchy. Successive Scottish monarchs had found bishops to be an excellent way of controlling their subjects. Presbyterianism, by its rejection of bishops, eroded that control. Unlike England, Scotland had become a Protestant nation not because her monarch had said so, but rather against the will of her monarch. In religious matters at least, the Scots saw the Kirk, not the king, as having the final word.

Presbyterianism challenged the natural pyramid of society. The king sat at the top, and power was supposed to flow down from the monarch, via his bishops and the clergy, to those who were sitting in the pews. Presbyterianism challenged that order by giving power to the people at the bottom. Ordinary people appointed their elders and their ministers, and then they met collectively in what was effectively an anti-parliament. Presbyterian power flowed from the bottom up, rather than from the top down.

Charles I (unknown artist after Sir Anthony Van Dyck).
Courtesy of the National Portrait Gallery, London.

This new brand of Christianity emphasised decision-making according to the 'Will of God'. The question was: who was best qualified to know the Will of God? Those who had been to university and studied divinity! This was a direct challenge to the King, as he had done neither. It is not surprising that he felt that Scottish Presbyterianism was affording him an inferior position.

This new philosophy was not likely to go down well with any monarch, but least of all with Charles I, Stuart King of both Scotland and England. Comfortably ruling all of Britain from London, he believed that God had appointed him King, and he was not about to be lectured on religious matters by misguided fanatics from 'up north'.

Charles I had been born in Dunfermline in 1600, but left Scotland when he was very young. Unfortunately, his Scottish birth left him with the delusion that he understood the Scots. By the time he succeeded to the throne in 1625, he had been cocooned from Scots and Scotland for almost his entire life, apart from his contact with a few obsequious Court Scots. Essentially, Charles I ruled Scotland through his 'yes men': his bishops. He heard only what he wanted to hear about Scotland.

From the very start of his reign, Charles appalled Scottish Presbyterians with his gross insensitivity. His coronation at St Giles', in Edinburgh, in 1633 was a masterpiece of arrogance. With bishops in full robes, it seemed designed to be a demonstration of how things ought to be done. This attitude alienated the Scots, and the coronation horrified radical Presbyterians, who did not like this kind of flummery. They saw Charles's coronation as a step back to the 'bad old days' of Catholicism.

But if the Scots were horrified by Charles's penchant for 'smells and bells', he was equally appalled by the starkness of Presbyterian churches – and shocked by the Presbyterian habit of allowing anyone at all to get up and pray out loud!

Charles was, himself, Protestant, but the Anglican Church he was used to south of the border was an Episcopalian world of bishops and ceremony. It was a far cry from this land of bare churches and passionate religious practices. Seventeenth-century Presbyterianism was a religion of the heart, not the head, and its practitioners enjoyed an ecstatic spiritual relationship with God.

One of the best examples of this type of religious adherent, and one of Presbyterian Scotland's most committed and prominent figures, was a young Edinburgh lawyer called Archibald Johnston of Warriston. Johnston was to become a key player in Scottish political and religious life.

In his diaries, he recorded in great detail his feelings and religious experiences. He wrote about everything from how he felt about his wife to what he had for breakfast. He recorded his prayers and the conversations that he was having with God – all in broad Scots.

Johnston's impassioned writing provides supporting evidence to those who claim that he was a manic-depressive, or that he was emotionally disturbed. But he was a highly intelligent Edinburgh lawyer with a deep personal piety. Prayer was the very core of his life, and he poured out his deepest thoughts and feelings to God.

King Charles I, however, had a very English sense of what was orderly and proper. Presbyterian worship seemed messy and even a bit seditious to him. He decided that what the disorderly Scots needed was a proper prayer book, with set prayers, just like the one that they had in England. To the Scottish Presbyterians, however, this sounded like watered-down Catholicism. It was the cue for a good old-fashioned Scottish 'rammy'.

Charles's attempt to impose his new prayer book was a fundamental mistake. For many Scots, who had got used to a far freer form of spiritual expression, the idea of having to mouth words that had been written down by bishops was completely unacceptable. It was not just a political or organisational point: they believed that using the prayer book would put their immortal souls in peril. Protestant Scots expected to go to hell if they could not freely communicate with their God and, as a result, the prayer book caused chaos.

While some Presbyterian ministers fell in line with the King's demands, many foresaw trouble ahead. Among them was the Reverend Robert Baillie. He was an astute and influential intellectual, and loyal to Charles I. Unlike many of his fellow ministers, he was not averse to the concept of bishops, but

New Service Book.

he could sense the gathering gloom. He noted in 1637: 'I am sore afraid that there is a storm raised which will not calm in my days . . .'.

When Baillie was presented with the new prayer book, he refused to read from it. He was widely considered a rather curmudgeonly old conservative; and, when the conservatives in a society start to rebel against their king, it is clear that the king has gone too far. But King Charles failed to read the signs.

Baillie's refusal to read from the prayer book was well judged. Other ministers were not so astute. Dean Hanna of St Giles' in Edinburgh must have had a sinking feeling as he got up to go into the pulpit on 23rd July 1637. The kirk was packed, and there was muttering and some heckling. Then the weeping and wailing started. Finally, someone threw the fateful stool. This was the cue for all hell to break loose. Stools came at the Dean from all directions. Barbara Mein, a respectable merchant's wife who had previously been known for her piety, led a mass walkout.

It is clear that, when Charles attempted to make Scottish worship more like the English, he did not realise how completely unacceptable this would be to the Scots. Perhaps this was just naivety on Charles's part; more likely, it was arrogance. He actually thought that they would allow a king living in London, and a handful of politically motivated bishops, to subsitute a foreign prayer book for their personal map of salvation.

Following the incident in St Giles', with popular feeling now behind them, Scottish Presbyterians responded to the King's meddling with an extraordinary act of defiance: the National Covenant.

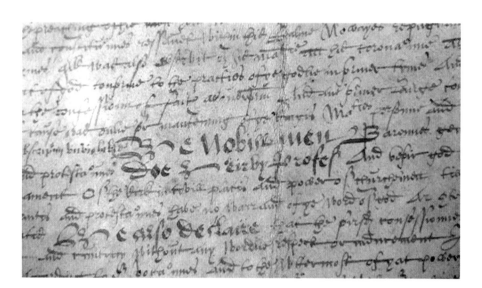

National Covenant.

A covenant is a promise or a contract which you enter into with God for all eternity. It is unbreakable and it is unassailable. It is remarkable not only that the Scots entered into this special relationship with God, but that they produced an actual document that Presbyterian Scots then signed. It was a unique moment, not only in Scottish but in European history.

The National Covenant was a written pledge to be signed by every adult male Presbyterian on behalf of himself and his household to fulfil their personal responsibility to God, and to defend Presbyterian practices. This explosive document was drawn up by the unlikely pairing of a minister and a lawyer – the minister was the Reverend Alexander Henderson, and the lawyer was the brilliant and deeply pious Archibald Johnston.

As far as Johnston was concerned, the King's claim to be Head of the Church was ungodly arrogance – only Christ, himself, could lay claim to that role. And, although not explicitly anti-monarchy, the National Covenant was a stand against the King's designs on Scotland's faithful, even if it meant armed resistance by the people.

The Covenant was both a religious and a legal document. It was cunningly couched in terms of loyalty to the King, in the sense that loyalty to God was seen as loyalty to the King because, of course, the King would not want to disobey God. The Covenant was clearly stating what the Scottish Presbyterians believed, what they stood for and what they would fight for.

The only way such a pledge could work was if everyone with a stake in society was involved. A national oath to God, which bound all parties forever, had to include everybody. Women were equally bound by the Covenant, although it was usually the men who signed on their behalf. The Covenant also cut across boundaries of wealth. It was, perhaps, an unplanned by-product, but the Covenanter movement was astonishingly inclusive.

The National Covenant was first signed in Edinburgh on 28th February 1638, and people came out to sign it in huge numbers. Copies of the Covenant were then sent across Scotland by horseback messengers. There were, of course, large tracts of Scotland that did not embrace Presbyterianism and did not care to sign the Covenant. Catholics and Episcopalians in the Highlands and in the North-East were resistant; but, in the areas where Presbyterian preachers had been at work, people came out in their droves. Within months, thousands had signed it, and, in signing it, they became 'Covenanters'.

The National Covenant was certainly an outlet for people's resentment of English interference, but it also caught the wave of the Reformation's invigorating zeal. The potent new symbol of the Covenant fuelled a new depth of personal engagement with Christianity at every level of society.

Ministers insisted that all Covenanters should understand the scriptures for themselves, which meant a push towards widespread literacy. At meetings, anyone, from noble to washerwoman, could pray and make himself or herself heard. Never before had there been such a force for the involvement of ordinary people in worship.

This kind of piety had a genuinely subversive element to it: God, it seemed, for reasons best known to himself, had not picked only the upper classes to have this intimate communion with him. In fact, God seemed to be passing out his favours in all directions – to weavers and shepherds and servants.

For the most committed, the Covenant touched every aspect of life. Archibald Johnston, torchbearer of the Covenanters, drew up a new version of the Covenant for his family each of the thirteen times his wife had a child. The whole family were signatories to this oath to God. The intensity of this kind of commitment could be uplifting and intoxicating, but it could also bring upon the faithful fierce psychological pressures of a less healthy nature.

It is difficult for us now to imagine a society in which people had such a strong belief in heaven and hell that it shaped so much of their lives. People truly believed that someone who had not had a conversion experience would go to hell. So, what were they to think about their children? Generally, it was believed that, if young children died, they would go straight to heaven as 'elect' infants. The dangerous time came when the children reached puberty. Teenagers were a cause for worry, both to their parents and themselves. Some young people sat awake at night, screaming and crying, for fear that they were going to hell. It was a life of enormous intensity, and people lived their lives at an extreme emotional pitch. Inevitably, many people found it hard to cope.

Archibald Johnston's own family suffered terrible mental traumas. When his son slipped into insanity, Johnston suspected that it was God's judgement on his *own* sins of pride and ambition. There had to be a reason behind everything. He attempted obsessively to find divine logic in every event from the 'trivial' to the 'tragic'. If the family cat vomited, it was a mark of either God's will or the Devil's!

This, then, was the universe of Presbyterian Scotland: people were galvanised into the extraordinary Covenanter movement in response to Charles I's bungling insensitivity. Far from bringing religious uniformity, his clumsy arrogance had caused a backlash of staggering proportions.

Unfortunately, instead of accepting that he'd made a mistake and trying to resolve matters, Charles proceeded to make things worse. He tried to buy time by calling a General Assembly of the Church of Scotland. For the Covenanters, this was a momentous opportunity to right the wrongs that had been done. At the Assembly in 1638, they denounced royal supremacy in Church matters and abolished bishops in Scotland.

In response, Charles declared war on the Covenanters. But, plagued by bitter disputes with his English Parliament, Charles could not, himself, finance an effective army. Nevertheless, he ignored the danger signs and marched an ill-prepared force north, knowing that his only hope was to scare the Scots into submission.

Archibald Johnston was very much in favour of military resistance, noting: 'They have neither Christian nor Scottish hearts who will expose their religion, their country, their neighbours, or themselves to present danger, without taking part'.

Inscription in Greyfriars Kirk, marking the spot where the National Covenant was signed.

Every available man was called up to defend the Covenant, the ranks swollen by experienced Scottish fighters returning from service overseas. Quickly bringing anti-Covenant Scottish cities to heel, a formidable Covenanting army lost no time in preparing for battle with Charles.

As military chaplain for a Covenanter regiment, Robert Baillie was torn. For a conservative, taking up arms against the King's forces was deeply unpalatable. His first duty, however, was to uphold the Covenant. If the only way the King would learn the error of his ways was through bloodshed, then so be it.

The opposing armies amassed, muskets and swords at the ready. However, on the very brink of battle, events took an unexpected twist. Facing a disciplined and skilled Covenanter army, and knowing his own forces were weak, Charles had second thoughts. He halted his troops at the Border, and stalemate rather than bloodshed ensued.

But if Charles thought that he had got away with his warmongering folly, he was in for a shock. After a year of uneasy truce between Scotland and England, the Covenanters invaded England and took the battle to the King. The disorganised rabble of Charles's army scattered before them. God was surely with the Covenanters!

The Scots had, audaciously, taken the initiative. Their army quickly moved south and took Newcastle and Durham. Charles was shocked. He had seen the Scots as a bunch of barbarian ruffians: this organised invasion was not supposed to happen. He had overlooked the significant number of Scottish officers who had come back from the Thirty-Years War to take part.

The Covenanters were victorious as Charles's army scattered before them.

These men had served as mercenaries, but had come came back to Scotland when they heard the clarion call of the Covenant.

For Charles, things were going very badly indeed. His armies were losing, and he was running out of money. These financial problems finally obliged him to call a Parliament in England, but this gave an opportunity to all those people who had pent-up grudges against Charles to express their resentment. It was a chance for grievances to be aired and political scores to be settled. The King was on the back foot in Scotland, and in the thick of political tension in England. To make matters worse, in Ireland the Catholic population declared that they were rebelling against the government 'in the name of the King'.

This really damned Charles in the eyes of his English parliament. They concluded that the King and the Irish were in league against them, and that, unless they made common cause with the Protestant Scots, the Reformation would be overturned, and Catholicism restored. The result was the Civil War.

Unbelievably, in a mere handful of years, the Covenanters had gone from being a niggling thorn in Charles's side to being the catalyst in his downfall, and a turning point in history. And they knew it.

The Covenanters' Mistake

With the chaos of the Civil War came an unmissable opportunity for the Covenanters to fulfil their ambitions, and they seized the moment.

In 1643, as the war raged, a handful of key Covenanter leaders left for London to negotiate with the English Parliamentarians. With them they took a radical deal that – they hoped – would secure the futures of both their Kirk *and* their State.

What the Scots proposed was that they would support the English Parliamentarian war effort, and fight on their side, in return for religion being brought into line across Britain. Their plan was that the English would adopt Presbyterianism and, as a result, there would never again be a situation in which an English government could try to impose bishops on Scotland. By exporting the Presbyterian revolution south, the Covenanters would not only consolidate Presbyterianism in Scotland, but they would also be England's salvation. Here was a golden opportunity to do God's work – and the Covenanters grabbed it with both hands. The agreement they entered into was called the 'Solemn League and Covenant'.

It was, effectively, a deal in which if England would accept Presbyterianism and the entire Covenanting agenda, in return, the Scots would put their army

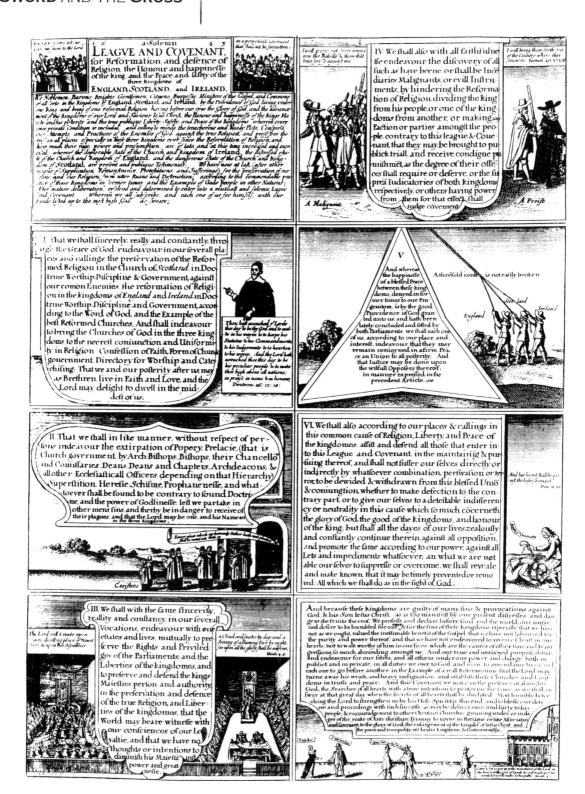

The Solemn League and Covenant of 1643, engraved by W. Hollar (1607–77) (engraving)
(b/w photo) by English School (seventeenth century). Private collection/Bridgeman Art Library.

at the disposal of the English Parliament. This, of course, was extremely bad news for King Charles. He was doomed from this point onwards, because he now had *two* large armies opposing him.

For the Covenanters, the agreement promised the ultimate prize. In return for the Covenanter muscle that would ensure victory for the Parliamentarians, this new covenant stipulated 'a reformation of religion in England, according to the word of God and the examples of the best reformed churches'. By which, of course, the Scots meant 'Presbyterian'.

Protestantism in England was still taking shape; the Solemn League and Covenant would ensure that the English Church would embrace Presbyterianism. The practicalities of how it would be put in place would be worked out later. An assembly at Westminster would fine-tune the agreement. In the meantime, there was a war to win.

There seems to have been considerable arrogance or naivety on the Scots' part. They did not consider the possibility that anyone might disagree with them. They sincerely believed that, when the best Scots preachers were sent to England, it would become obvious to everyone that they ought to adopt Presbyterianism.

This was a deeply ironic but very dangerous moment for the Covenanters. Only a few years before the outbreak of the Civil War, Charles I had hopelessly misjudged Presbyterian Scotland by thinking he could impose English Church practices. It had led to no less than revolution. Now the Covenanters were attempting to impose Scottish practices on England.

But soon the Covenanters found themselves fighting on two fronts: against Charles to the south *and* against Scottish Royalists from the

Highlands. Tens of thousands were dying on all sides, in battle or from disease and hunger.

There were numerous stories of atrocities on both sides, which only fuelled the hatred that each had for the other. The warring factions were united only in their religious bigotry, and in the depth of their hatred towards one another. Looking back from our twenty-first-century vantage point, we can see that they were no different from anyone else in Europe at that time. For those looking down the barrel of a gun, however, that knowledge was unlikely to have been of much comfort.

Out of this bloody turmoil, one Englishman was rising to dominate the English Parliamentarians: Oliver Cromwell. He was a formidable military commander; and, with the help of the Covenanters, the war was swinging in his favour.

Oliver Cromwell was a Puritan who shared many religious beliefs with the Covenanters; but an uncomfortable realisation was dawning on them:

Covenanter.
Photograph: David Quinn

Cromwell had no intention of enforcing Scottish Presbyterianism across England. The kind of theocracy the Scots wanted would have been intolerant of the very groups who had supported Cromwell politically. It was beginning to look as though the Parliamentarians would renege on their side of the deal. At this point, however, the war took an unexpected turn. With Cromwell's troops hot on his heels, Charles I found himself seeking refuge with the Covenanter army.

Statue of Oliver Cromwell, Westminster.

This may seem a bizarre turn of events, but Charles had calculated that, while the Covenanters might have rebelled against him, in principle at least, they still pledged allegiance to him as monarch. The Parliamentarians, on the other hand, wanted rid of him completely. On this occasion, the Scots were the lesser of two evils.

Not surprisingly, the Covenanters were embarrassed to have Charles turn up on their doorstep. Anxious not to antagonise the English Parliamentarians, and lured by the promised £400,000 in unpaid fees for their part in the war, the Covenanters handed Charles over to the Parliamentarians in the winter of 1646. 'Traitor Scot sold his King for a groat' was the English jeer.

But for a while, the future looked bright for the Covenanting regime in Scotland.

Many Presbyterians were uncomfortable that their King was in Cromwell's custody; but, with the King safely tucked away, the Covenanters took the opportunity to create in Scotland the Presbyterian State that the Reformation had promised them.

Oliver Cromwell (1599–1658) (oil on canvas) by Gaspar de Crayer (1584–1669).
Chateau de Versailles, France/Bridgeman Art Library.

They were, in effect, setting up the Republic of Jesus Christ. The Covenanters' firm belief that they were living in the last days before the Second Coming of Jesus Christ influenced their every move. Just as people tidy their houses before a guest arrives, they were cleaning out the rubbish before the arrival of Jesus. And 'the rubbish' was anyone who disagreed with them theologically.

It was essential that Scotland was a godly and perfectly reformed country, and the ministers of the Kirk were convinced that they had God-given authority to discipline Scotland. The Covenanting ministers tried to stop people getting drunk, going out dancing and committing adultery. Church attendance was enforced. The image of the 'killjoy' Presbyterian dates from this time.

On the other hand, these same radical ministers had a great concern for the education of ordinary people. They were keen to ensure that children went to school and that they learned to read the Bible. The Covenanters' rule was certainly characterised by severity and intolerance, but regimes born out of extreme violence do tend to be intolerant – and short-lived. And this one was no exception. The Covenanting regime was soon rocked by deeply shocking news. While they had been happy to hand over Charles I to the Parliamentarians, the Covenanters had never expected the news that came to them from England: Cromwell had executed the King.

It might seem contradictory that, after challenging the King, the Scots were deeply shocked by his execution, but the Covenanters did not want Charles to be killed. They wanted him to repent and change his heart, to accept the Covenant and return as their King.

The Scots had two great points of national pride: one was that they believed themselves to have the best reformed religion in the world; the other was that they had the oldest monarchy in the world. They now asked themselves: 'If we don't have a King, do we really have a constitution? What sort of nation are we?' The monarchy was important to their sense of history and identity, and Cromwell's act of regicide caused profound anxieties in Scotland.

So, just three days after the execution of Charles I, the Scots declared his son 'King Charles II'. But, safe in exile in the Netherlands, the young Charles II needed some convincing.

Charles II (unknown artist, c.1648). Courtesy of the National Portrait Gallery, London.

Robert Baillie was one of the leading Covenanters sent to persuade the young heir to the throne that the Scots genuinely wanted him as their King – provided, of course, that he agreed to sign the Covenants. Baillie was probably aware of how it looked for the Covenanters to be going cap-in-hand to the son of the monarch whom they had unwittingly sent to the axe, barely months before. He and his more extremist colleagues also knew, however, that young Charles had little option. If Charles II wanted any power, however meagre, he would have to agree to the Covenanters' agenda. And so, on a nervous trip to Scotland, Charles II reluctantly signed the Covenants and became puppet King of Scotland.

Oliver Cromwell, now head of the English Parliamentarian army, was furious about this expression of loyalty to the Crown. He had barely disposed of one King, and the Covenanters had brought in another! Cromwell's response was swift. He invaded Scotland.

The Covenanters' defences collapsed with pathetic swiftness. They had been conquered by the same forces with whom they had so recently been allies. With a hostile English army on his tail, and thinly disguised disdain for the Covenanter regime he had sided with, Scotland's new King, Charles II, fled back to the safety of the Continent.

The hopeless military rout at Cromwell's hands split the Covenanters. Bitter recriminations were traded about who had been responsible for their abject military failure. It was a spiritual conundrum as well as a political one. How could their God have allowed Scotland to be conquered? They, who had perfected themselves under the Covenant – how could this have happened to them?

Praying.

There were two schools of thought. The 'godly' maintained that they had not been pure enough; that, in fact, what they should have done was purge themselves of all ungodly persons. If they had done this, God would have blessed them. The more worldly Presbyterians held to a different interpretation: they thought that they should have made political alliances with all sorts of other people in order to succeed in their aims.

Both groups of Covenanters tried to curry favour with Cromwell.

Heading the political camp was a smooth-talking negotiator, the Reverend James Sharp, minister of Crail. Sharp, the ambitious son of a sheriff clerk, had risen quickly through the ranks of moderate clergymen, thanks to a gift for diplomacy and a talent for networking.

Rising to prominence within the uncompromising godly camp was the extremist, Archibald Johnston. He and Sharp became bitter enemies, vying for influence with Cromwell in London. A Puritan who had much in common with the radical Covenanters, Cromwell naturally favoured Johnston's camp over Sharp's. The Presbyterian State that Cromwell tolerated in Scotland had a place for Johnston.

But, barely seven years after the conquest of Scotland, Cromwell died.

With Cromwell gone, it became clear that only his own fierce grip had held the Parliamentary regime together. Without him, England faced near-anarchy. Cromwell's death exposed the fragility of his regime: his failure to put in place a viable alternative to the monarchy had left the way open for Charles II to succeed to the throne.

Initially, the Covenanters took this to be good news. Certainly, they had handed over Charles I to the Parliamentarians; but the fact that the new king, Charles II, had signed the Covenants surely marked the beginning of a bright new era for Presbyterians. Sadly, for them, this was not to be the case.

The Covenanters were hopelessly weakened by their eagerness to please the restored monarch, now back from the Continent, this time as all-powerful King of Britain. Loyalty to Charles II now determined the fates of the Covenanters and their leaders.

Baillie, the moderate, was content to serve the King. As a reward for his acquiescence, he was appointed Principal of Glasgow University. Sharp, the sly negotiator, did even better. He was sent by the Covenanters to plead their case at Charles's court – but, to their horror, he returned as the Episcopalian Archbishop of St Andrews. It was a staggering betrayal that would not be forgotten.

Sharp's rival, Archibald Johnston, the Covenanter firebrand, was not so lucky. He had colluded with Cromwell, the very man who had executed Charles II's

Statue of Charles II, London.

father. Only one possible fate awaited Johnston – death. Royal propagandist spin could not have hoped for a more pitiful figure: here was the fearsome torchbearer of the Covenant, begging for mercy on the scaffold, unable to recognise his own children, sobbing that he had forgotten the Bible.

At the end, Johnston asked his enemies to repent, and then said goodbye to his family and 'dear Scotland'. Johnston was hanged, his head hacked off and displayed in Edinburgh for all to see.

The Killing Times – Charles II's Revenge

The true extent of Charles's intentions soon became clear: he wanted revenge. Charles cancelled all the legislation that the Presbyterians had put in place in Scotland. The Covenant was declared illegal, and all the ministers who had been ordained since his father's execution had to seek reordination. He brought bishops back. He eliminated the Covenanters' revolutionary leaders. Charles was squeezing the life out of the Covenanter movement.

At least, that is what he thought he was doing. Out in the countryside, however, trouble was once again brewing. Rebelling against the reimposition of bishops, one third of all the ministers simply walked out of their churches. Thousands of Covenanters – ordinary people – defiantly left their church pews and followed their ministers into the wilds. As Charles tightened his grip on the Covenanters, the most faithful of them slipped through his fingers and into the hills.

*A Field Conventicle, 1857,
by Paul Falconer Poole
(1807–79).*
Phillips, The International
Fine Art Auctioneers, UK/
Bridgeman Art Library.

Outdoor gatherings of the faithful began to spring up across the Scottish countryside like an epidemic. These were called 'conventicles'. People would pass around the details of where and when they would meet by word-of-mouth – rather like an illegal rave today. They would meet on the moors, miles from anywhere.

As time went by, more and more people joined the rebel Church movement. At some conventicles 10,000 people met in defiance of royal authority. In the south-west of Scotland, the boycotting of official church services became so rife that the government sent in the military to impose fines on non-attenders. And they were free to extract fines any way they could. The Covenanters' outdoor worship was declared illegal, and troops began arriving to break them up. Fines and imprisonment rained down on those who refused to budge, but this had little effect on the recalcitrant outlaw ministers and their flocks.

When the government troops became over-zealous, and an elderly man in the village of Dalry was threatened with horrific torture, the local Covenanters took matters into their own hands. They seized the soldiers and raised an army to march on Edinburgh. However, the Covenanters were disorganised and badly led. At Rullion Green in the Pentland Hills, they were defeated, and hundreds were taken prisoner.

Archibald Johnston's old rival, royal lapdog James Sharp, exercised his new powers as Archbishop mercilessly. He called for the prisoners to be executed as traitors. This act sealed his turncoat reputation, and he became probably the most hated man in Scotland.

But the crackdown did not stop with the more radical Covenanters. Moderate Presbyterians also began to suffer from a widening campaign of persecution. Being a Presbyterian could stop your getting work. They were treated as a despised, second-class group. Those who lived in strongly Presbyterian areas would be likely to find troops quartered in their homes. The troops would eat them out of house and home, steal anything they could find, and even rough people up.

These were reasons enough for the moderates not to want to be associated with the extremists; but soon even the semblance of brotherhood was to be extinguished. The extremist struggle was about to rise to a whole new level.

On 3rd May 1679, a band of armed Covenanters on the prowl near St Andrews stumbled unexpectedly across the reviled traitor Archbishop Sharp, travelling by coach. Whether by chance or, as they believed, by God's will, here was an outlet for the Covenanters' fury. In front of his terrified daughter, Sharp was dragged from his coach and shot, and stabbed repeatedly.

The Crown came down hard and fast. Sharp's assassins were caught and executed, and royal troops scoured the Lowlands in search of illegal conventicles, in the hope of stamping out remaining pockets of resistance.

Conventicles took place in rural locations.
Photograph: David Quinn

The assassination of Archbishop Sharp.

Expecting only the tattered remnants of the faithful, weakened by constant harassment and violence, what they found came as something of a shock. The Covenanters were more than ready to fight back. Swelling the ranks of experienced soldiers from the Civil Wars was a *new* radicalised generation, ready to die for their cause. These were young men who had grown up knowing only persecution – they had nothing to lose.

These far more militant Covenanters included among their number a young university student called William Cleland. He was widely travelled and an enthusiastic poet. Nevertheless, at Drumclog in Lanarkshire, Cleland found himself making more of a mark with his musket and sword than with his quill.

At the conventicle at Drumclog, when word came that the dragoons were closing in, a well-oiled plan was put into action. The minister led the women and children to safety and the men turned to fight. The government troops had expected to come across a group of desperate people on the run. What they found was a conventicle lined up for battle. Many Scots had served either in the Civil Wars or abroad – and, led by Cleland, they were victorious, much to the horror of the authorities.

For the Radicals, victory at Drumclog was proof that God was once again with them in their struggle. Unfortunately, for these Covenanters, it was to be a short-lived victory. At the battle of Bothwell Bridge in 1679, less than two months after Archbishop Sharp's assassination, the radical Covenanters were resoundingly defeated. Hundreds of prisoners were taken after the battle; they were marched to Edinburgh and herded into tiny

The Radical Covenanters defended the right to hold conventicles.

enclosures in Greyfriars Kirkyard – still known today as 'the Covenanters' Prison'.

The government did not want to release people it saw as subversives back into general society. Those who were seen as the most radical and dangerous were executed in the nearby Grassmarket. For the rest, there was another solution: transportation to the colonies. This was before Australia had been set up as a penal settlement, and so this sentence meant transportation to America, virtually as slaves. Many of the prisoners from Greyfriars were manacled and put on board a ship which sank off Orkney. The prisoners were not released. Nobody helped them. Almost all of them drowned.

However, this was not the end of Covenanter resistance, and the bloodiest phase of all was yet to come. The remaining Radicals, William Cleland among them, split into cells called 'Societies', each made up of ten to twelve Covenanters. The Societies were highly secretive, and had little

The Covenanters' prison, Greyfriars Kirkyard.

knowledge of other cells. They had a secret – but not very inspired – password, which was 'Reformation'. The forces of the State pursued the Radicals vigorously. Cleland was already a veteran of Drumclog. Now, at just eighteen years of age, he was an outlaw.

With their cell structure and young, determined recruits, the Societies were successful in eluding Charles's forces – but they were simply buying time. Eventually, they decided to band together. The 'United Societies' issued a series of increasingly extreme ultimata. It was a declaration of total war on the State. They believed that the King had no place in religious matters, and they urged all Scots to stand up against his ungodly rule.

The Societies remained in their mountain hideouts, drafting protestations and manifestos, and writing political tracts. Even to the Covenanting Radicals, they seemed extreme. But they were pursued relentlessly by Charles II, and many were executed. This policy of high-profile executions, however, simply created more legends of glorious Covenanter martyrs. Realising this, the Crown changed its policy.

In 1684, the government brought in the 'Abjuration Oath'. This was cunningly framed to single out extremists and identify them for execution. If you were caught out in the open and you refused to take the Oath, you were simply shot on the spot. It was low-profile, simple and effective. And it marked the height of the 'Killing Times' in Scotland.

The Covenanters' fierce defence of every individual's direct relationship with God had been their greatest strength. The most radical of them were willing to die for it, without hesitation. But their refusal to compromise their beliefs and engage with political realities was also their greatest weakness. One by one, they were hunted down. Then, in 1685, with the Covenanters on the very edge of oblivion, their relentless persecutor, Charles II, suffered a stroke and died.

The Covenanters' prison, Greyfriars Kirkyard.

James II and VII (unknown artist).
Courtesy of the National Portrait Gallery, London.

The Last of the Covenanters

Charles was succeeded by his Catholic brother, James VII and II. It would be logical to assume that a Catholic King would mean even less chance of the Covenanters surviving. In fact, ironically, it would ultimately secure their future.

Protestant England was terrified by the prospect of James restoring Catholicism. A faction within the English parliament took extreme measures: they invited Protestantism's Dutch heavyweight, William of Orange, to take the throne in order to thwart James. With his eye on the British Crown, in 1688 William swept into England without resistance. In Scotland, however, the situation was somewhat messier.

The Highlands, which had always resisted Presbyterianism, had no intention of giving up their new Catholic King. In the glens, the Jacobites prepared to halt William's advance.

Predictably, riding to the defence of William of Orange, came the Covenanters. The forces of the infamous United Societies under William Cleland undertook a suicide mission to hold the line against the Jacobites at Dunkeld. The religious and political fate of Scotland was balanced on a knife-edge. If the Jacobites broke through at Dunkeld, the Lowlands would swiftly fall to Catholic James. It was to be the Covenanters' last stand.

Dunkeld was the scene of bitter street fighting.

Under Cleland, 1,000 Covenanters took up positions among the houses and the cathedral. However, on 21st August 1689, it became painfully clear that they were hopelessly outnumbered by the Jacobite force. Jacobites began to force their way through the heavy musket fire levelled at them from the cathedral, taking the houses around it.

Before long, the Covenanters were out of ammunition. They had begun to strip lead from the roofs to make more musket balls – when the Jacobites' *own* ammunition ran out.

The hand-to-hand fighting that followed has become the stuff of grim legend.

Early in the battle, Cleland was shot in the head and liver. Mortally wounded, and concerned for the morale of his troops, he tried to crawl away, out of sight, so that his troops would not see him, dead. He need not have worried. With

Photograph: David Quinn

brutal efficiency, his Covenanter forces blocked the Jacobites in the houses they had taken, and set light to them.

With no ammunition, and no shelter to fall back to, the remaining Jacobites retreated. Against all odds, the Covenanters had won the Battle of Dunkeld. The Highlanders disappeared back into the glens, their army finished. Any effective resistance to William of Orange's advance into Scotland was gone, and Catholic

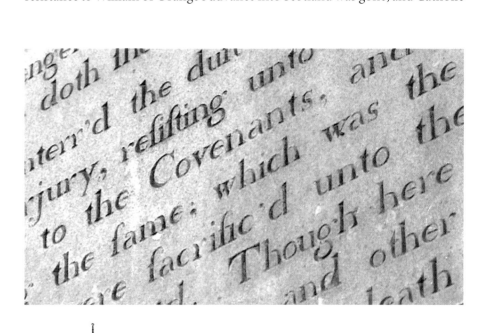

James was ousted as King. The last of the Radical Covenanters had decided Scotland's fate.

After fifty years, four kings, a revolution, a Civil War, military occupation, countless dead, and a reign of terror that almost finished them, the Covenanters had achieved what they had been fighting for. With Protestant William of Orange in power, the Presbyterian Kirk of Scotland became the established church.

Soon, the supporters of the ousted King James found that it was, once again their turn to face intolerance. Episcopalians and Catholics across Scotland would endure religious and political persecution in the years that followed.

Within the Kirk, it was the Presbyterianism of the moderate Covenanters that prevailed; but there is no doubt that the legacy of the Radicals has shaped Scotland – and not only in religious terms. The Covenanters' insistence on education and their hunger for knowledge paved the way for the great flourishing of philosophy and science in the century that followed: the Enlightenment. Those who subscribed to the Covenanters' style of piety were committed to observing the world closely. They believed they would see God's providence exemplified in it. And while ecstatic, internal, experience was important for them, they also observed the outside world minutely. They believed that the universe was fundamentally explicable. Even Archibald Johnston's diaries, for all their strangeness, represent an experiment in knowing and understanding the world. Almost to the very end of his life, through all the chaos and suffering of the Civil War, Johnston was obsessed by the idea that the world could be explained.

The Church of Scotland Assembly Hall: the first home of the Scottish Parliament.

Most importantly, in their struggle against royal power and patronage, the Covenanters' influence on the relationship between the State and the citizen still resonates to the present day.

When Scots were searching for a political language for Scottish constitutionalism, they instinctively reached back to the Covenanters. When the Scottish Parliament was being set up, trade unionists, ministers and politicians all gathered together and signed 'the Claim of Right'. This was a document that came straight out of the Covenanting struggles of the seventeenth century. For, regardless of a person's faith, the National Covenant can still be seen as an inspirational document. Using a secular interpretation, it represents ideas of civil responsibility that remain valid today. It reminds us of the importance of standing up and being counted, of taking on authority, of challenging governments that are clearly out of line, governments that are exercising State terror.

Greyfriars Kirk today.
Photograph: David Quinn

In an age that is sceptical of religious claims, it is hard to understand the passion of the Covenanters. They were people for whom the meaning of life was obedience to God in this world, and enjoyment of him in the next. They believed they could gain a direct and personal knowledge of God's divine purpose for them, both as individuals and as a nation. And, as we have seen, they were willing to die for those beliefs.

But they were also willing to challenge the arrogance of royal power – 'divine right' – and, in breaking that power, they helped to bring in the modern age. And, in that sense, we can say that it was their blood that bought our freedom.

PART 4

THE GODLY COMMONWEALTH

On a misty June evening in 1935, a hostile crowd of more than 10,000 Protestants surrounded a Roman Catholic priory where the congregation was celebrating Mass. The mob made their feelings very clear: 'No to Rome. No to the Antichrist!' Through a loud hailer, their leader rallied his troops: 'Rome is the Dominion of Darkness. Its seed shall not take root here in our soil.' As the Mass ended, policemen created a diversion to allow the Catholic worshippers to slip out by the back door, and onto waiting buses. But members of the crowd spotted them, and they surged forward, forcing the buses to run the gauntlet of the baying mob.

We became familiar with such events during the Northern Irish 'Troubles', but these events took place not in Ireland but in Scotland – in the Morningside district of Edinburgh. At this time, Scottish Protestants genuinely believed that their culture was being swamped by what they saw as a flood of Irish Catholic immigrants. And some prominent Kirk leaders had been only too ready to fuel their fears. Since the early 1920s, they had pursued a campaign to marginalise Catholics of Irish descent, in a vain attempt to return to a golden age of Presbyterianism which had ended over a century before.

Upsetting the Balance of Church and State

At the end of the eighteenth century, Scotland found itself in the grip of revolution – the industrial revolution. Industrialisation was rapid, and towns were growing at an unprecedented rate. The Church of Scotland, which had been the nation's spiritual and moral guardian since the time of John Knox, sensed disaster ahead.

Tartan on loom.

Vast numbers of people were moving from both Highland and Lowland rural parishes to the new urban industrial areas to work in factories. The existing parish structure in the towns was simply unable to cope with this great influx of people. The Kirk's control over its flock – and its ability to care for it – was being strained to the limit.

In the towns, housing conditions were appalling, but the town councils' first concern was building factories and making profits. The physical, moral and spiritual welfare of workers came far down their list of priorities. The Kirk, of course, was deeply worried, but it lacked the resources to intervene. The problem was that, in the growing towns, the churches were controlled by the town councils.

When the Presbyterian Church had been created in 1560 out of the upheaval of the Reformation, Scotland had been a rural society. The countryside was divided up into a network of small parishes, each run by a minister who was responsible for both the welfare and the discipline of his parishioners. The parish church, with its kirk session of elders and minister, was at the heart of the whole life of its community. It provided poor relief to those households that

*Ken Currie, 'Weavers'
Struggles . . . The Calton
Weavers Massacre', Panel 1.
Oil on canvas, 218 x 251 cm.
Glasgow Museums:
The People's Palace.*

had lost their income as the result of the death of a loved one. It also provided the local schoolmaster. When there were social problems that, today, would be dealt with by social workers, it was the minister and the kirk session who stepped in.

The kirk session was also constantly on guard against sins such as fornication and adultery, drunkenness and swearing. Guilty parties had to pay a fine and, sitting on the penitent's stool in church, they had to accept a public rebuke from the minister. In a stable, rural society, this had proved a very effective way of regulating the behaviour of ordinary people; but, in the towns and cities, the parish system was stretched to breaking point. It just was not possible for the

Church to keep a watchful eye on the vast numbers of new people flooding into the towns. The Kirk was losing control – and it feared the worst.

Then the worst happened. When, in 1787, weavers in the Calton district of Glasgow went on strike over pay-cuts, civil order collapsed. The town council locked the weavers out of their factories, and the weavers responded by tearing down the looms of 'scab' workers and burning the looms in the street. As trouble spread, the city magistrates called in the army. The result was nothing short of bloody mayhem.

The riot of the Calton weavers was the first to hit the booming cotton industry in Glasgow, and it was the most violent the city had ever seen. Six protesters were killed, and their leader was flogged and banished. To many in both Church and State, it signalled a massive breakdown of social discipline.

The Kirk believed that, at the heart of the failure, was a lack of spiritual guidance and discipline. It identified as crucial the fact that children as young as four were being made to work from early in the morning until late at night, six days a week. With no time for schooling, they were unable to read, and, if they could not read, they could not understand the Bible. And if they could not understand the Bible, they had no access to the moral and spiritual instruction that the Church provided.

Five days after the Calton weavers' riot, a minister of the Kirk proposed to Glasgow town council a novel way of cooling the hot heads of young apprentices on their one day off work – Sunday school. This may seem to us today to be an unlikely way of curbing revolutionary fervour, but, by teaching children how to read and write, the Kirk believed that it could shape their beliefs and, therefore, control their behaviour.

Burning loom on brazier.

Thomas Chalmers, by David Octavius Hill (and Robert Adamson), 1802–1870. By courtesy of the National Portrait Gallery, London.

Within months, Sunday schools were to be found all over Scotland. The new schools kept children busy between 8am and 7pm. As well as providing them with a basic education, Sunday schools also kept them out of mischief on their day off. They were a runaway success and soon Sunday schools became part of the social fabric of Scotland.

However, the creation of Sunday schools was just the opening salvo in the Kirk's campaign against moral decline. The stakes were high: the Kirk faced being sidelined as an increasing irrelevance in a modern, industrialised world. Sunday schools alone would not be enough. So the Church decided that the battle had to be taken to the authorities of council and government who had been responsible for allowing the urban rot to set in. The man to take up the cause was an enthusiastic Evangelical minister, the Reverend Thomas Chalmers.

Thomas Chalmers was born in 1780 in Anstruther in Fife, the sixth son in a family of fourteen. An intelligent boy, he became a student at the University of St Andrews at the age of 12. He was a fine mathematician, but eventually chose to study theology, with a view to becoming a minister.

By accepting the call, in 1814, to be minister of the Tron parish church in Glasgow's city centre, Chalmers took up the challenge presented by Scotland's new industrial society, and, in the process, he was to change the course of the Kirk's history.

Chalmers was horrified by the conditions he found in Glasgow. Everywhere he looked, he saw poverty and despair. The town councils did not seem to care about the welfare of the workers, and the Church, which *did* care, did not have the resources to act. Chalmers feared that social unrest would be the inevitable consequence, if something were not done soon:

> On looking at the mighty mass of a city population, I state my apprehension, that if something be not done to bring this enormous physical strength under the control of Christian and humanised principle, the day may yet come when it will lift against the authorities of the land its brawny vigour and discharge upon them all the turbulence of its rude and volcanic energy.

Chalmers had good reason to be fearful of a revolution that would overthrow the existing social order, and, possibly, overthrow Christianity itself. He was working in Glasgow in the 1820s, barely thirty years after the French Revolution. He would have to do something about the situation. But doing something about it would not be easy. At the time of the Reformation, the Scottish Parliament had fully supported the idea of a Protestant nation. By the nineteenth century, however, Scotland was in the thrall of the Westminster Parliament, and, from the beginning, Westminster had meddled in Scotland's religious affairs.

In 1707, when Scotland and England had united to create 'Great Britain', Parliament had given Scottish town councils the right to choose ministers and to control the churches within their boundaries. The move had deeply upset the Kirk, but the last time the Kirk had challenged the State, that confrontation had led to fifty years of bloody warfare.

Fearing a return to the Killing Times of the seventeenth century, the Kirk had backed off at the time of the Union and had agreed to council control.

High Kirk of St Giles', Edinburgh.

Now, Thomas Chalmers believed that it was time, once again, for the Church to rise up and challenge the State. Chalmers and his supporters could see that order in the towns was close to collapse. If the town councils could not keep up with the rate of change in society, then it was up to the Church to step in and do the job for them. If the State would not act, then the Church would have to rescue society.

And not for the first time. At the Reformation, John Knox had attempted to transform Scotland by creating a whole new sense of Scottish identity based on Presbyterianism. In what Knox called the 'Godly Commonwealth' – a vision of national unity based on shared values and beliefs – Church and State would work together for the good of the people. The State would be responsible for the collection of taxes and the defence of the realm, but the

Kirk would take charge of the discipline and education of the people. The result would be a perfectly ordered, harmonious society, with the Kirk at its heart.

It was this vision of a Godly Commonwealth that drove Thomas Chalmers. His strategy was to set up new parishes in the urban, industrial areas. The Church would move into the new communities, look after their welfare, and address the pressing need for poor relief. Chalmers would employ a rural parish model in the new urban industrial setting.

Statue of Thomas Chalmers, Edinburgh.

He set about organising the construction of 220 much-needed new churches in the towns. Church members financed the building work; but, once the work had been completed, Chalmers expected the town councils to pay to maintain the new churches.

But if he had hoped that they would fall into line with his plans, he was in for an unpleasant surprise. The councils refused to maintain the new churches. By the early nineteenth century, the British State saw itself as representative of all the people that lived within its borders, and this included large numbers of people who were not members of the Church of Scotland. Perhaps as many as a third of the population were Protestant dissenters or Roman Catholics, and the State realised that those people would have been marginalised within Chalmers's Godly Commonwealth.

Chalmers was furious. He felt that the State was caving in too quickly to those outside the Kirk. If the Godly Commonwealth were to succeed, the councils had to be on board. By their refusal to co-operate with the Kirk, the councils had, in effect, thrown down the gauntlet. Chalmers had done what he could to regain control of the 'heathen' in Scotland's cities. Now it was clear to him that, if the Kirk were to press forward with its reforms, it would have to challenge the State itself.

But the government could see what Chalmers could not – that Scotland was becoming a diverse nation. The State could not be seen to support one Church at the expense of others, no matter how powerful that Church might be. All Chalmers could see, however, was the State obstructing his plans.

And there was another reason for his anger. In the Spring of 1838, the court of Session had declared the Veto Act illegal. This was an Act which had allowed congregations to veto an unpopular patron's choice of candidate for a parish living. The State was primarily concerned that the candidate and the patron should be treated fairly, but for Chalmers it was the last straw. It seemed to him that the State wanted to retain the right to interfere in the Kirk, but was unwilling to give the Kirk the resources it needed to meet the needs of the people of Scotland.

The Disruption

Chalmers was now determined that the Kirk would regain control of its own affairs. He felt he had no choice:

> Amid the illusions and momentary visitations that conscience provokes, let us never, never lose sight of the test, that by their fruits ye shall know them . . . When conscience calls, we must act with one accord to bring about that state which is ordained by God for all humanity. To ignore this call of conscience would be to ignore God and to turn our backs on the truth.

Reading the Claim of Right document.

In 1842, Chalmers drew up a document known as the 'Claim of Right', demanding that the Kirk be granted complete independence. He wanted the Church to choose its own ministers, to fund its own poor-relief schemes, to educate its own children, and to build its own churches. In effect, he was initiating divorce proceedings against the State. Parliament, however, was not interested in any quickie divorce. It refused even to consider the issue. To the dismay of Chalmers and his supporters, the 'Claim of Right' was rejected.

*St Andrew's and
St George's Church.*

As it was clear that the State would not readily give up its control of the Church, Thomas Chalmers felt that he was left with only one choice. Reluctantly, he made a decision that was to see him both vilified and canonised by later generations of Presbyterians. In 1843, he set the stage for a final confrontation between Church and State at the Kirk's annual gathering in Edinburgh – the General Assembly.

The extraordinary events of 18 May 1843 were to become known as 'the Disruption'. By the time the doors of St Andrew's Church on George Street in Edinburgh – the venue of that year's Assembly – opened to the public at 5am, people had already been queuing for some hours. Rumours had been circulating that something momentous was about to happen. As the pews

*Stained glass, St Andrew's
and St George's.*

began to fill up with members of the public, anxious to get a ringside seat, the tension in the air was palpable.

The first act of the day was a harbinger of things to come. In the throne room at Holyrood Palace, leading nobles and clergymen were meeting with the Lord High Commissioner, the Crown's representative at the General Assembly. As they were about to leave, a portrait of King William III, the architect of the so-called Glorious Revolution that had finally guaranteed a Presbyterian Scotland, came crashing to the floor. With heavy hearts, the cortège made its way to St Andrew's Church for the real business of the day.

The portrait crashed to the floor.

Once everyone had gathered, the Moderator of the previous year's Assembly, Dr David Welsh, rose to his feet:

> We protest, that in the circumstances in which we are placed, it is, and shall be, lawful for us and such other Commissioners chosen to the Assembly appointed to be this day holden, as may concur with us, to withdraw to a separate place of meeting for the purpose of taking steps, with all who adhere to us, maintaining with us the Confession of Faith and Standards of the Church of Scotland, for separating in an orderly way from the Establishment.

As Welsh and Chalmers bowed respectfully to the Lord High Commissioner, their supporters got to their feet and, in sombre mood, they began to file out of the chamber, one pew at a time. From the public gallery, people looked on in stunned silence as the implication of the events they were witnessing slowly sank in.

Chalmers and Welsh led the departing ministers out of the church and along the street in a procession that was a quarter of a mile long. Thousands of onlookers lined the streets, scarcely comprehending what they were seeing. Despite the many ups and downs of their relationship in the previous 300 years,

Photograph: David Quinn

no one had really believed that the stormy marriage of Church and State would ever end.

The procession made its way to Tanfield Hall in the Canonmills district of Edinburgh, but, on arriving at the venue, Chalmers's worst fears were realised. Not only had there been a disruption of the relationship between Church and State, the Church itself had been disrupted. As they assembled in the Hall, Chalmers saw that only one third of the clergy had followed him out – about 400 ministers of the Church of Scotland. Crucially, two thirds of the ministers had remained behind. While an enthusiastic crowd cheered him to the rafters, it began to dawn on Chalmers that the unthinkable had happened – the national Church had just torn itself in two.

Chalmers was devastated. Within a couple of hours, however, he and his followers had constituted themselves as the new Free Church of Scotland. They immediately convened their first Assembly, and Chalmers was appointed as the new Church's first Moderator.

In the following weeks, the ministers and lay members of all the churches recently built by Chalmers came out en masse as members of the new Free Church. In Aberdeen, all of the ministers declared for the new church. In Glasgow, it was twenty-five out of forty. In the Highlands, where the Clearances had been driving poor crofters from their homes, they joined the new body in their thousands. Chalmers's boldness had captured the imagination of Scotland.

But the Disruption of 1843 was both a tragedy and a triumph for Chalmers and his vision of Scotland as a Godly Commonwealth. It was a triumph inasmuch as it was an assertion of the spiritual independence of the Church from the State.

But, at the same time, it was a tragedy because it split apart the one institution that was capable of delivering the vision of a Godly Commonwealth – a truly national Church with a presence in every parish.

But while the new Church may have proved popular with ordinary people, the government was not pleased with what had taken place. It immediately challenged the legal validity of Chalmers's Free Church of Scotland. A House of Lords ruling dispossessed the new body of its church buildings, claiming that they were still the official property of what was left of the Established Church.

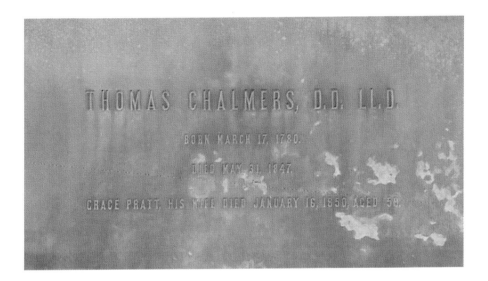

It was a tactic that Chalmers had expected. In its long history, the Presbyterian Church had been here before. Whenever ministers and congregations had been thrown out of their buildings during the Covenanter Wars, the people had taken to the hills and the fields to hold their services. And, just like those who had gone before them, Chalmers's new flock met on beaches, in woods, on boats – anywhere that the authorities could not prevent them from gathering. Nothing could quench the spirit of the new Free Church of Scotland. And soon there was a new rhyme on the city streets:

> The Wee Kirk, the Free Kirk, the Kirk without the steeple;
> The Auld Kirk, the Cauld Kirk, the Kirk without the people.

Immediately after the Disruption, the Established Church of Scotland fell into a low state. Many of the most talented and most zealous members had left. Of those who remained, many were feeling hurt by the rhetoric of the Disruption, and were prepared now to go along with the State. Scottish Presbyterianism

Thomas Chalmers, by David Octavius Hill (and Robert Adamson), 1802–1870.
By courtesy of the National Portrait Gallery, London.

THE **SWORD** AND THE **CROSS**

had been permanently damaged. Where formerly there had been one strong national Church, there were now two. It was not long before the new Free Church rivalled the size and power of the old Kirk. Within five years, the Free Church had built 730 churches, 500 schools, and 400 manses. It had virtually taken over the Overseas Mission of the Established Church, and embarked on an aggressive programme of urban mission in Glasgow and Edinburgh. It was an astonishing feat. Chalmers had hoped that, by doing so, he might revive the Godly Commonwealth through the New Free Church, but, in reality, both churches spent the years that followed duplicating each other's efforts and squandering resources.

In his desire to create a Godly Commonwealth, Chalmers's actions had, ironically, put it forever beyond his grasp. His dream of the Godly Commonwealth was dead.

Chalmers died in 1847, just four years after the Disruption. At his funeral, the streets of Morningside were lined with thousands of people from both the Established and non-Established churches. What he had achieved had been a truly national revolution. But it had been at huge personal cost. To dissolve the formal link between the Church and the State was one thing – but to shatter the unity of the Church itself was something he had never intended.

That is the paradox at the heart of Thomas Chalmers's life. He set out to change Scottish society, but he ended up changing the Church. He crippled the Church, just as it was about to face the challenges of the new Scotland that would emerge by the end of the nineteenth century.

Sectarianism

No sooner had the Disruption torn the Kirk apart than another disaster happened which was to weaken further a now-wounded Protestant Scotland. Between 1846 and 1850, a disastrous potato blight hit Ireland, causing the worst famine the country had ever known.

The potato crop, the staple diet of the rural peasantry of Ireland, had failed, and almost one and a half million Irish people either starved to death or were forced to emigrate. While many of them set sail for America, thousands of others came to Scotland in search of food and work. And, with their arrival, came a major resurgence of Roman Catholicism.

Despite the Protestant Reformation of the sixteenth century, Catholicism had never completely died out in Scotland. In the Highlands, pockets of the population had remained strongly Catholic. Neither was immigration a new

ATURDAY, MARCH 23, 1929.

For even the most
ill agree that the police-
has for so long been an
pful, and ever-watchful
streets and lanes that
surrounded him with a
ess and good faith. No
course, that the police
nposed of supermen, to
of the flesh common to
м are unknown. The
the first to acknowledge
this respect. The state-
Report, therefore, that
ion do occur is neither
in the nature of a
h the records of recent
before it the Commis-
ave done otherwise than
does upon this point.
vindicates the morale of
ouches for the sterling
he vast majority of

that corruption and
es do occur, the Report
e for these can some-
on the doorstep of the
precisely by its censure
cedure that the Report
. The police constable
a man and an officer,
l rules he defends and
wn to be in certain
d of reform. In most
endations the Report
nes of the Savidge
rity Report. Both
and that police officers
ments from witnesses
ur to avoid visiting
place of work, and
hould have the option
ds and legal advisers
where the attendance
to no objection. Both
is no evidence of the
Degree methods. The
Report goes further,
recommends that the
nen police should be
that legislation should
that would allow of
being inspected. This
important. The public
agree with the Commis-
the practice of sending
to night clubs disguised
olly objectionable and
ibited. The suggested
amed in such a way as
nt of search and inspec-
a better ethical footing.
ny world, however, one
reason, whether people
type could ever be
playing honest cricket.
g and deep question in
ical philosophy, and it
e how the police, who
instrument for safe-
liberty of law-abiding

IRISH IN SCOTLAND

Inquiry Into the Facts

EXTENT OF ROMAN CATHOLIC INCREASE

HIGHER MARRIAGE RATE

Further striking evidence of the rapid multiplication in Scotland of descendants of former generations of Irish immigrants is given to-day in the fourth article of the series dealing with the threat to Scottish nationality of the growth of the racially-Irish element in the community.

It is shown that in the 40 years from 1881 till 1921 the Roman Catholic population in Scotland, composed to the extent of over 90 per cent. of members of Irish extraction, increased from 327,000 to 601,000. On a conservative estimate the total Roman Catholic population in the country to-day is put at 650,000. Upwards of 450,000 of these are resident in the Glasgow diocese, in which the Roman Catholics represent 23 per cent. of the inhabitants.

In an analysis of the marriage rate it is brought out that there are now, taking Scotland as a whole, two Roman Catholic marriages in every 15, whereas some 40 years ago the ratio was two in 20.

IV.—THE CONCERN FOR THE FUTURE

BY OUR OWN CORRESPONDENT

What is really the numerical strength of the Scottish residents of Irish extraction? In my last article I estimated that the whole Roman Catholic communion in Scotland would number about 650,000 out of a total Scottish population of roughly 4,900,000. That represents a proportion of 13.26 per cent. of Roman Catholics in the country—not in itself an alarming encroachment on the Protestant predominance in the nation, which is still left with 4,250,000 members of the Reformed Faith, less Jews and that small minority of the agnostic and the ecclesiastically unplaceable. Not alarming, I say—if the balance were not undergoing a constant modification in favour of the Catholics by the faster augmentation of their progeny. That is the disturbing aspect for those who are concerned in this connection about the national future. The increase in the number of Catholic school children and the maintenance of a relatively high birth-rate in the Catholic community mean almost inevitably that succeeding generations will see a deeper and deeper sinking of the wedge, which is already some little way beyond the insertion of the thin end. Still, it is somewhat premature, I think, for Scottish Protestantism to give way to an end-of-all-things pessimism.

Catholics 90 per Cent. Irish

The only way to get at the number of the racially-Irish colony in our midst, Scottish-born and Irish-born together, is to measure it as a great preponderance of the Roman Catholic population. The Church of Scotland rather weakened their case, in my opinion, by insisting in effect that there is no difference—that Irish and Roman Catholic in this regard are synonymous. The Church Committee were so near the truth that it would not have done their argument any material harm to have made the slight

times the rate of increase of all others in Scotland. A century ago they were 1 in 30 of the population; in 1921 they were 1 in 8."

The criticism, of course, might be offered that this is reducing comparison to an absurdity, by going back for a datum line to a time before the Irish emigration movement to Scotland had well begun.

Estimates of the Catholic Total

In putting the Roman Catholic population at 650,000—almost 600,000 of them of Irish descent—I am estimating conservatively. The computation of the Scottish Churches Council in 1926 was that the total then had reached 640,000—and whatever may be said of their inferences it must be admitted that the Council's statistics are generally worthy of the utmost respect. The Church and Nation Committee of the Church of Scotland went a little farther. In 1927 they calculated the "Irish population" (using Irish as an interchangeable term for Catholic) at "more than 650,000, and probably nearer 700,000," their suggestion being that it would require the higher figure to embrace those who had lapsed from the Catholic communion. On this point of lapsed membership I was given to understand that the Roman Catholic Church does have this problem, but in a much less aggravated degree than the Protestant Church. From 10 to 15 per cent. of Catholics drift away from the Church, generally in the frivolous and reckless period of early manhood and womanhood, but the estrangement is as a rule only temporary. When the careless ones come to assume matrimonial responsibilities nearly all of them return to receive the Church's blessing on their union and to have their children born within the pale. For the rest of their lives they remain loyal.

Recent Headway

It may have been the thought of these lapsed members who would return later to the bosom of the Church that prompted

The Glasgow Herald.
23 March 1929. Courtesy of the Mitchell Library, Glasgow.

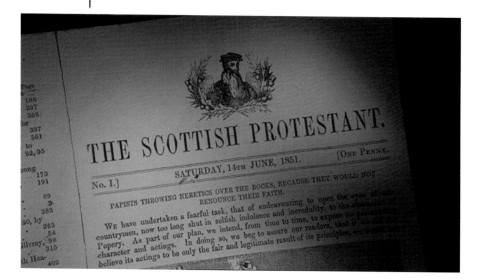

The Scottish Protestant
newspaper.

thing – Irish Catholics had been making their presence felt in Scotland since the beginning of the nineteenth century. This, however, was different.

For although Irish Catholics had been coming to Scotland to work as seasonal farm labourers and as textile workers, their numbers had been relatively small. It was not until the onset of the famine that immigration really escalated. For the first time in 300 years, it looked as if Catholicism might again become a major influence on the Scottish nation.

In the period immediately after the famine, the Scottish establishment became increasingly concerned by the extent of Irish immigration, for social reasons. But, in addition, some from the more extreme wings of the Protestant Church, and particularly the Free Church, became concerned for theological or denominational reasons.

Since the Reformation, the Kirk had continued to think of the Pope as the 'Antichrist', and the Catholic Church as something which had been banished forever from the Godly realm of Scotland. To its horror, the 'Antichrist' had just returned.

Reaction was immediate and extreme. A series of anti-Papal meetings was organised across Scotland, and many petitions were sent to Parliament, denouncing the menace of 'Papal aggression'.

Anti-Catholic newspapers such as *The Scottish Protestant* emerged, expressing, in the strongest terms, grave concern about the arrival of the Irish and the return of Roman Catholicism:

> If the hopes of Popery to regain her dominion of darkness in this
> kingdom of light are beginning to revive, it is because she is colonising

our soil from another land with the hordes of her barbarised and enslaved victims whom she proudly styles her subjects.

Despite a generalised hostility towards the arrival of the Irish, this kind of organised sectarianism was confined mainly to Glasgow and the West of Scotland. For the next few decades, simmering resentment and prejudice remained, largely, under the surface.

The issue that, eventually, made manifest the huge divide between Scotland's Protestants and Scotland's Catholics was one that struck at the very heart of Presbyterianism – education. The spark that ignited the bonfire was the Scottish Education Act of 1918. With an increased demand on its resources, the Catholic Church in Scotland had been struggling to finance its schools. Many were oversubscribed, and many more had insufficient qualified teachers. The Catholic Church turned to the government for help.

The Presbyterian Churches were furious. They saw education as a means of instilling in the Scottish population a sense of their Protestant identity. Now, not only had Roman Catholicism regained a foothold in Scotland, but Protestant taxes were to be used to pay for Catholic education.

Both the Established Church of Scotland and Chalmers's new Free Church had opted into the State education system in 1872 when the State had made education compulsory for every child between the ages of 5 and 13. In return for full funding by the State, they had given up their rights to control the curriculum and to run their own schools.

But the agreement the Catholic Church secured in 1918 gave it much more control. The Catholic Bishops agreed to transfer their schools to the State sector under three stipulations. First of all, Roman Catholic clergy would be allowed full access to schools. Secondly, there would be religious instruction. Most importantly of all, the Catholic Church would have a view about the character and background of those teachers appointed to teach in Catholic schools. While not every teacher in school had to be Catholic, the Church had to approve every teacher.

The Protestant Churches were deeply envious, and not a little resentful. They

Barony Church, Glasgow.

might have been divided on other issues, but they agreed that the unchecked advance of Catholic education, funded by the State, was an outrage. They complained bitterly that this was 'Rome on the Rates' – and a threat to the very identity of the Scottish nation.

In an increasingly acrimonious propaganda war, the Protestant Churches accused the Roman Catholic Church of being the enemy of Great Britain and, more significantly, of being in league with Germany. The reality of the situation, however, was very different, and the State knew it. Millions of British subjects had died in the World War that had so recently engulfed Europe, and the British Catholic population had suffered and died for their country just as British Protestants had done. In Scotland, the Catholic Bishops had fully supported the war, and many Scottish Catholics had volunteered to fight in the trenches.

So, as one war ended, another was beginning, and Scotland's unsuspecting Catholics were to find themselves at the very heart of the conflict. Fighting with them side by side in the trenches had been the man who would now turn his attentions to Scotland's Catholics – a young Church of Scotland army chaplain by the name of John White.

As a chaplain, White had served with the Cameronians at the Battle of the Somme. His reputation had been good: a caring chaplain who was concerned for his men, and prepared to go into the front lines to carry the wounded back to safety. Little did the Catholic troops who had fought at the Somme realise that John White would become the next Protestant general in the battle against Roman Catholicism.

Irish republic proclamation.

White wanted to reclaim for Presbyterianism a Scotland free from what he saw as the evils of Catholicism.

But, as a result of the Disruption, the Church of Scotland's troops had divided into two rival Protestant brigades. White knew that an army divided against itself could not stand: he had to reunite the two main Presbyterian Churches.

John White had been appointed minister of the Barony Church in Glasgow in 1911, but it was only after the First World War ended that he set out to resurrect the dream that had died at the Disruption. He hoped that if the Free Church and the Established Church were to reunite, it would breathe new life into the idea of the Godly Commonwealth.

He believed that a country that had just been through the horrors of war, and was now faced by massive social and economic challenges, would be ready to welcome the Kirk back to its rightful place at the heart of Scottish society. His vision of a reunited national Church echoed Thomas Chalmers's vision of the 1830s and 1840s. Both men thought that a national Church would ensure the well-being of Scotland, and John White really believed he could make Chalmers's dream a reality. But, unlike Chalmers, who had lived through the period when Scotland's economy was booming, White was ministering to a country in economic decline.

So, shortly after the First World War, the Presbyterian Churches decided on a Mission of National Rededication to focus on the rebuilding of Scotland as a Protestant nation under God. It was the opening salvo in White's campaign to rescue Scotland for Presbyterianism.

Then, John White was appointed Joint Convener of a newly-established body in the Church of Scotland: the Church and Nation Committee. This Committee's remit was to examine 'the duties of the Church in regard to the life of the nation'. As far as White was concerned, the biggest threat to the nation was the continuing influx of Irish Catholics. While Thomas Chalmers had been a champion of Catholic emancipation, believing that Roman Catholics might be converted and drawn into the Godly Commonwealth, John White recognised that there was no way Roman Catholics could ever be included in his vision of a Presbyterian nation.

The public's attitude to the Irish also had been slowly hardening again. Towards the end of the First World War, the Irish Republican Army had used Britain's difficulty as their opportunity. They had attempted to establish an Irish republic through yet another rebellion. In Dublin, they had been defeated by the British army, but, for many Protestant Scots, this attempted Irish rebellion had been an act of outright treason.

If the Irish were traitors, then their very presence was a threat to national unity. White demanded that the General Assembly investigate the extent of Irish Catholic settlement in the West of Scotland, and a committee was set up to look into it. That committee's report on what it called 'The Menace of the Irish Race' was presented to the General Assembly of 1923. Looked at from our twenty-first-century perspective, it is a truly shocking document:

> . . . Would the Irish race, would the Church of Rome, welcome the incursion of half a million Scotsmen into the country of Dublin? God placed the people of his world in families. And history, which is the narrative of His providence, tells us that when kingdoms are divided against themselves they cannot stand.

Large numbers of people sympathised with White's views. In the 1920s and 1930s, many people thought in terms of racial categories in a way that we would regard today as entirely unacceptable. They embraced ideas that we would now describe as Social Darwinism. People thought about culture, society and politics in terms borrowed from biology. There was a great deal of talk about 'racial characteristics', and the whole western world was in turmoil over the same issues. In America in 1925, 40,000 Ku Klux Klansmen marched down Pennsylvania Avenue to proclaim white superiority over the nation's black population. In Germany, the Nazis were trumpeting the strengths of the pure Aryan race at the expense of the nation's Jewish population. In Scotland, the racial scapegoats of otherwise respectable establishment men like John White were Roman Catholics of Irish descent.

White assumed, as many people did then, that cultural and social characteristics were racial – that they came with your blood. If a group of people displayed a certain characteristic – for example, being illiterate – they would always have that characteristic, and they would export it to wherever they moved. That was the basis of his argument in describing the 'menace' of the Irish. He was not aware that those kinds of characteristics are largely a matter of environment, and that they can change very quickly indeed.

In late 1925, White rallied his troops and went on the offensive. His committee claimed that 9,000 Irish Catholics per year were flooding into Scotland and, like locusts, were stripping Scotland bare of its public and private relief funds. In addition, the presence of so many Catholics was in danger of derailing the destiny of the Scottish race, which, for him, must be a Protestant destiny.

The Glasgow Herald – *'Reunion of Christendom', 4 October 1929. Courtesy of the Mitchell Library, Glasgow.*

REUNION OF CHRISTENDOM

Lord Davidson on Importance of Scotland's Part

ROME THE STUMBLING-BLOCK

CLOSING ADDRESSES OF MODERATOR AND DUKE OF YORK

There was again a great gathering, and few empty seats in the vast area of the Hall, when the Assembly of the Church of Scotland resumed in the evening for the final session.

Lord Davidson, the former Archbishop of Canterbury, addressing the Assembly, declared that the Scottish Union was of distinctive importance in the world-wide effort towards the goal of a reunited Catholic Church.

He instanced the Roman Catholic Church as the principal difficulty in the way of reunion. "They will tell us that the footpath is easy if we will do their bidding," said Lord Davidson, "but . . . . we can enter no portal of fellowship which has 'submission' graven on its lintel."

The Duke of York, in his farewell address, also struck the note of larger unity.

The Moderator appealed to the Church to guard the Union by using it to the utmost for its great purpose and causes, and to weld it more firmly by an open trust of one another and forbearance with one another on the little differences they had carried up with them.

THE CHURCH AND THE MODERN WORLD

The Right Rev. Dr John White, the Moderator, was again in the chair. On his right and left sat the ex-Moderators, Dr Mitchell and Principal Martin. The Lord High Commissioner (His Royal Highness the Duke of York) and the Duchess occupied the royal throne, attended by their suite.

The Rev. Dr Henry Sloan Coffin, president of Union Theological Seminary, New York, addressed the Assembly on "The Church in the World of To-Day." He said that the outstanding contrast between the world which the Church confronted to-day and the world of a relatively recent past was the disappearance of Christendom and its replacement by a secular civilisation whose sole reliance was in man. This disappearance of Christendom was not all loss. Some of the beliefs and much of the ethic deemed Christian they now recognised hardly merited the name. The Church had been compelled to restudy the gospel of Christ, to scrutinise its implications for those who professed it, to ask what must be their programme for human society if it was really to become Christendom—a world after the conscience of Jesus Christ.

braced the majority of the Christian people of Scotland. That was an invaluable advantage. Its congregations ought to cement in comradeship folk of every class and temperament and degree of culture, and redeem them from mutual suspicion and misunderstanding, from snobbishness and offishness. Such congregations should prove brotherhoods which created similar friendly relations between employers and employed in industries, between various classes in their communities. The Christendom which once was was now gone, for worse and for better. A secular civilisation reliant solely on men swayed wellnigh the whole globe. A worshipping and teaching Church bravely manifesting the life of her Lord in the morally adventurous lives of her members, and supplying an earth-wide fellowship to exemplify the unity of mankind in Christ and link the peoples in one, might under God create a genuine Christendom pervaded by the faith and love of its Lord. (Applause.)

THE NON-CHRISTIAN WORLD

Mr J. H. Oldham, speaking on "The Call of the Non-Christian World," said those who had been privileged to take part in the acts constituting the united Church or to witness them must go away with a deepened sense of the meaning of history. What was the character of the world in which the work

healing and repair has far greater meaning and significance than it might have in other lands.

Every Scotsman has for generations more or less understood for himself questions which would be quite unmeaning to ordinary folk elsewhere.

If you will pardon a personal note. I was myself, in year not far after the Disruption, brought up in Scotland, and though I flitted early across the Tweed for training and education and wo c quite another kind and allegiance I have vivid memories of the talk of my elders in those days, and had heard of Auchterarder and Strathbogie long before I can have had a glimmer of what they stood for, and I regarded it as a kind of adventure when I was taken once in a way to listen to such men as Candlish and Guthrie at their best. Such memories come flooding in upon me now.

THE STANCE AT LAMBETH.

But it is no of Scottish Church history that I am asked to speak to-night. You have had that before you to the full in these crowded days. I want to cast my eyes with you over a wider field.

For twenty-five years it has been my privilege to hold in the Church of God a position which is nearly—not quite—unique. The man whose stance is at Lambeth has opportunity of looking out upon the Christian world in all its parts, and fashioning high hopes as to what may come to pass in Christendom in the decades or centuries that are to come. Of course we can all of us do that, but I have had opportunity beyond most other men. As things stand the Archbishop of Canterbury is in ceaseless contact with those who hold the Christian faith and lead Christian followers in all parts of the world, say on the banks of the St Lawrence, or on the shore of the Bosphorus, or on the Danube, or the Elbe, or the Euphrates, or the Ganges or the Nile. Such has been my daily task for more than a quarter of a century, and it has meant the task of trying under the hand of God to bring the sundered portions of the Church of Christ into harmony, or even to weld them into one.

CHRISTIAN UNITY

IF POSSIBLE, THEN OBLIGATORY

It is not, therefore, quite out of place that I should stand here to-night among responsible Christian men to say a word on the topic you have given me—Christian unity.

Christian unity. In the light of our Lord's prayer "that all may be one" that unity cannot be impossible, for if so, what means His prayer? and if it be possible, then surely it is obligatory.

Now I ask you what is our actual effort for it worth? Neither the thought nor the effort is new, but you and I are set to live in a decade of the world's life when the conditions are new. We have to face the new conditions resolutely and squarely, and so we will. Here is one new condition. Our ordinary secular world is becoming unified to a degree quite novel. What about our telephones, our broadcasts, our aeroplanes, and all the rest? They are in prosaic fact forcing peoples into one. Distance is getting annihilated. You "listen-in" this evening by your own fireside, and Paris, Berlin, Warsaw are all at your ear. That is an entirely new condition in the world's life, a condition which our grandfathers never dreamed of. Partition walls are crumbling away. In one sense there is unity perforce. We are simply crushed into it. If so, does Christian unity come in?

ONE CHRISTIAN BODY POLITIC.

Then another new condition. What does the League of Nations stand for? Of course, people can distrust it, but at the

The General Assembly was shocked by this alleged Papal plot to dilute the purity of the Scottish race. They responded in typical fashion by handing the issue back to White for further investigation. He began to compile detailed statistics on the numbers of Irish Catholics living in Scottish parishes and the kinds of jobs they did. It was not long before the other Presbyterian Churches were joining him in his campaign.

With a new common purpose – and a common enemy – the different Presbyterian Churches were becoming closer allies by the day. White's campaign to establish a Godly Commonwealth in Scotland was firmly on track. The golden age of Presbyterian rule was surely about to return. With increasing confidence, the Presbyterian Churches sent a joint delegation to discuss the Irish situation with the government.

At a meeting with the Secretary of State for Scotland, the Churches demanded legislation to curtail Irish immigration. White was hoping that the achievement of such a goal would demonstrate the potential power of a reunited Presbyterian Church of Scotland. As far as the State was concerned, however, the Churches were overstepping the mark. The Scottish Office had been doing its own research, and could prove that the Kirk's Irish immigration statistics were vastly over-inflated.

Quite simply, John White had misunderstood the numbers. He thought that there were far more people coming into Scotland than there were. He also failed to take account of the fact that around one third of those coming into Scotland were actually Presbyterians from Ulster. These immigrants were religiously and culturally very similar to the majority of Scots, and were absorbed very quickly into Scottish society, almost disappearing from sight.

But the Churches were blinkered by their own prejudice. As they finally agreed on a date for reunion, Scotland's newspapers decided to look for themselves at the churches' allegations about Irish migration. An investigation in the late 1920s by the *Glasgow Herald* demonstrated that Irish migration to Scotland in the 1920s had dwindled. This was not surprising, as Irish migration to Scotland was encouraged by economic forces, and in the 1920s and 1930s Scotland was certainly not an attractive destination, from the point of view of economic migrants.

But John White did have one cause for celebration: the momentum towards Church reunion had reached the point of no return. In October 1929, the Free Church and the Established Church finally reunited.

But if White had hoped that the reunified Church could impose its will on government, he was disappointed. The State had other ideas: it would not allow the Church to affect social policies such as immigration. Having

Daily Record and Mail, Wedn

Councillor Cormack's Policy

IF I WERE DICTATOR OF EDINBURGH

JOHN CORMACK, native of Edinburgh, virile, demagogic, started four years ago with 40 supporters to " reclaim Edinburgh for John Knox "; now assembles 4000 members in his Action Society. Town Councillor with eight colleagues; is fighting two seats this election (unorthodox but apparently with motive); young man of some influence.

His " dictatorship " policy is controversial. The *Daily Record* does not necessarily associate itself with his statement.

Dictator Cormack :—

First.—I want Edinburgh to be 100 per cent. Protestant. And I mean to get it. By municipal representation? Yes, the electors can do it, *are* doing it. But the Town Council is not interesting until I have the power.

Ah, but when I have the power! Let's look around this city's population. It is 91 per cent. Protestant, only 9 per cent. Roman Catholic. Am I beating about a harmless bush? Just nine per cent.

But see what would happen if I had my way. There would be a fairly generous clearance in Corporation

Councillor Cormack

employing departments—the tramways, cleansing, Burgh Engineer's squads.

There are unemployed Protestants. I would draft them in immediately. Of course, there are other Roman Catholics in Edinburgh. Leave them alone. I only want justice.

It might all seem vindictive, pandering a bit. There's more to it. Personally, I am anti-Catholic. More fundamentally, I hate the Catholic bloc vote. By whatever method, I mean to defeat it.

Triumphant March

Protestant Dictator Cormack! What would I do? Right off, demonstrate our triumphant Protestantism. I would call a great celebration march through the Capital, hailing our faith, rallying other cities.

Next, ally myself with the other cities in forcing the Government to repeal Section 18 of the Education (Scotland) Act. If I'm alone, I'll do it alone. I shall defy the Government.

I shall nullify all Roman Catholic ecclesiastical authority in the schools, appoint my own teachers.

I shall issue orders to all Protestant Churches in the city to carry out the vows they took upon ordination. Ministers failing to comply will be displaced forthwith.

I shall ban all outside demonstrations of Catholics, Fascists, Communists. Catholics must worship in their own churches, Fascists and Communists at their own pet corners.

Burn The Slums

I want a civic aerodrome. Transport of the future is by air. Edinburgh must be contacted with progress.

Subsidy or no subsidy, I shall burn down the slums, give no compensation to landlords of condemned property. In other cases it may be inevitable. I want drastic alterations in the transport facilities; the lesser routes scrapped; more buses, trolley buses.

Despite the costs, I shall build houses for the people. And quickly.

Probationer nurses would have a minimum of £42, first issue of uniform free. Maximum for nurses £120. And no stupid restrictions.

I shall fire the latent Protestant spirit in this city, make it a centre of truly Protestant culture. And Edinburgh will stir the world.

Give me five years. Less!

'If I were dictator of Edinburgh',
Daily Record and Mail.

at last achieved reunion, however, the newly emboldened Church was not about to accept its loss of influence quite so readily. The Kirk's policy towards Irish Catholics intensified. With unemployment on the increase, it accused Catholics of taking up the few jobs that there were. And on the streets, the masses were listening. This was the era of the Great Depression. In the early 1930s, the US stock market collapsed, along with most of the world's economy. If Catholics were truly the cause of this misery, people wanted to hear about it. It was not long before new anti-Catholic organisations emerged.

There were no direct ties between the Church of Scotland and the populist sectarian movements that became active in Edinburgh and the East of Scotland at this time, but the Kirk's views can only have helped to strengthen the populist anti-Catholicism that found expression on the streets. On the ground, a disillusioned public was listening closely to the reunited Kirk's anti-Catholic rhetoric.

*The site of the Morningside
riots of 1935.*

Soon the public's convictions were being translated into votes. In Edinburgh, a group called Protestant Action was set up by John Cormack, a former Black and Tan soldier. The Kirk's anti-Catholic pronouncements were music to his ears and, before long, Cormack was elected to Edinburgh Council as a member for Leith.

From the moment he took office, Councillor Cormack campaigned against the presence of Catholics in the nation's capital. In an article entitled 'If I were Dictator of Edinburgh', John Cormack wrote:

> I want Edinburgh to be 100% Protestant. And I mean to get it . . .
> I shall nullify all Roman Catholic ecclesiastical authority in the
> schools, appoint my own teachers. I shall issue orders to all Protestant
> Churches in the City to carry out the vows they took upon ordination.
> Ministers failing to comply will be displaced forthwith . . . I shall fire
> the latent Protestant spirit in this city, and make it a centre of truly
> Protestant culture.

When in June 1935 the Roman Catholic Church held its largest ever outdoor gathering in Scotland, the Eucharistic Congress, anti-Catholicism reached fever pitch.

Scotland's first Roman Catholic Eucharistic Congress, designed to stimulate the devotion of the faithful to the sacrament of Holy Communion, was held at Morningside in Edinburgh. It outraged Cormack, and he stirred up a mob to demonstrate against it. For three days, Cormack's supporters targeted Catholics attending the event. At a Catholic women's meeting in Waverley

Market, his Protestant mob attacked the car of the Archbishop, and pitched battles were fought through the night between rival crowds of Protestants and Catholics.

Then, on the last evening of the Congress, Cormack led a crowd of more than 10,000 Protestants to St Andrews Priory, where an equal number of Roman Catholics were holding an outdoor Mass. As the Catholic worshippers concluded their devotions, Cormack and his mob harangued them from outside the walls of the priory.

With the Mass drawing to a close, the police created a diversion, fooling the mob into thinking that the worshippers were about to leave by the main entrance. When it became clear that they were secretly leaving through a side exit, the furious Protestants charged their buses, smashing windows and threatening the terrified passengers. Four Protestant rioters were arrested, and many people were injured.

There was no direct link between the church's anti-Catholic stance and such acts of violent sectarianism. But, although the Church never advocated anti-Catholic violence, at the time, it did not publicly condemn it either. Very few ordained Church of Scotland ministers actually shared a platform with extremists such as John Cormack – but some did. And the anti-Irish propaganda instigated by John White in the previous decade, by a man who was, after all, twice Moderator of the Church of Scotland, was hugely influential. He created an atmosphere in which prejudice against Catholics was, at least, acceptable within the Church of Scotland. The uncomfortable truth is that White's campaigns gave sectarianism a veneer of respectability.

But while Scotland teetered on the brink of violence, on continental Europe, Germany was sliding into the abyss. Over two nights in November 1938, German Nazis began to purge their country of its Jewish population. Some 300 synagogues were burned and 7,000 Jewish businesses destroyed. All of these acts were carried out in the name of racial purity.

Events in Germany seem to have drawn Scotland – and the Church of Scotland – back from its own ethnic cleansing abyss. Furthermore, the shock of seeing the consequences of the kind of racist attitudes that leaders of the Church of Scotland had been explicitly, and complicitly, supporting in that period played out in Germany, sobered and silenced those voices.

The outbreak of the Second World War, ironically, gave Scotland a second chance. In September 1939, everything changed. As Germany invaded Poland, Protestant Action and other political fringe groups in Scotland were made irrelevant. With the threat of imminent Nazi attack, a new desire for national unity gripped the country. If the nation was to survive, both Protestants and Catholics were going to have to work, fight, and die together.

The Future for Christianity in Scotland

When the Second World War ended in 1945, it was not just Nazi Germany that had been defeated. The true horror of what Hitler had done to the Jews in the name of racial perfection would soon be revealed to the world. And the attitudes of Scotland's Protestants to their Roman Catholic neighbours was suddenly cast in a new and shameful light. The anti-Catholic campaigns of Church leaders such as John White, and politicians like John Cormack, were finally consigned to history.

Of course, although not as virulent as it was in the 1930s, there is still too much sectarian hatred in Scotland – even if it is now seen on the football terraces rather than at the General Assembly of the Church of Scotland. But is that malignant residue all that is left of 1,500 years of Christian history?

Certainly, since the 1960s, the tide has been going out on Scottish Christianity. Today, Scotland is a plural, largely secular society, in which the Churches have to take their chances, just like any other voluntary organisation.

Spirituality is not dead, of course, nor is the insatiable human appetite for the search for meaning in a mysterious universe. We are no longer impressed, however, by the great institutional expressions of faith – partly, because we

know how cruel they can be once they get power over us; partly, because we know that life is more complicated than they were ever prepared to admit.

But it would be wrong to suggest that Christianity was defeated in its long struggle with the State. If the State forced tolerance upon the churches, it was the churches that taught the State charity and compassion. The welfare state is the implicit Christianisation of society. Christianity's greatest triumph is to have bequeathed its own best values to the State that triumphed over it.

The Church's battle with its own soul, however, is far from over. So what can it learn from the violent struggles that have beset Scotland's Christian history? The lesson surely has to be that religion can be toxic unless it is lightened with humour and practised with love. The Church may discover that, although the people of Scotland have rejected it as a master, they may yet welcome it back as a friend.

BIBLIOGRAPHY AND FURTHER READING

Part 1

Adomnán of Iona: The Life of Columba, translated by Richard Sharpe, Penguin, 1995

Dauvit Broun and Thomas Owen Clancy (eds), *Spes Scotorum: Hope of Scots: Saint Columba, Iona and Scotland*, T&T Clark, 1999

Ewan Campbell, *Saints and Sea Kings: The First Kingdom of the Scots*, Canongate, 1999

Thomas Owen Clancy and Gilbert Márkus OP, *Iona: The Earliest Poetry of a Celtic Monastery*, Edinburgh University Press, 1995

Donald Meek, *The Quest for Celtic Christianity*, Handsel Press, 2000

Alfred P. Smyth, *Warlords and Holy Men: Scotland AD80–1000*, Edinburgh University Press, 1989

Part 2

Jane Dawson, 'John Knox', in the *New Dictionary of National Biography*, Oxford University Press, (forthcoming 2004)

Jane Dawson, 'The Two John Knoxes: England, Scotland and the 1558 Tracts' in *The Journal of Ecclesiastical History*, 42, 1991

Eamon Duffy, *The Stripping of the Altars*, Yale University Press, 1992

Rosalind Marshall, *John Knox*, Birlinn, 2000

Roger A. Mason (ed), *Knox: On Rebellion (Cambridge Texts in the History of Political Thought)*, Cambridge University Press, 1994

Margaret Sanderson, *Cardinal of Scotland: David Beaton c.1494–1546*, John Donald Press, 2001

Margaret Sanderson, *A Kindly Place? Living in sixteenth-century Scotland*, Tuckwell Press, 2002

The Works of John Knox in 6 Vols (Edinburgh, 1846–64)

Part 3

Thorbjörn Campbell, *Standing Witnesses: An Illustrated Guide to the Scottish Covenanters*, Saltire Society, 1996

James Robertson, *The Fanatic*, 4th Estate, 2000

Margo Todd, *The Culture of Protestantism in Early Modern Scotland*, Yale University Press, 2002

Part 4

Callum Brown, *Religion and Society in Scotland Since 1707*, Edinburgh University Press, 1997

Stewart Brown, *Thomas Chalmers and the Godly Commonwealth in Scotland*, Oxford University Press, 1982

Stewart Brown and George Newlands (eds), *Scottish Christianity in the Modern World*, T&T Clark, 2000

Steve Bruce, *No Pope of Rome! Militant Protestantism in Modern Scotland*, Mainstream, 1985

Tom Gallagher, *Edinburgh Divided: John Cormack and No Popery in the 1930s*, Polygon, 1987

Harry Reid, *Outside Verdict: An Old Kirk in a New Scotland*, Saint Andrew Press, 2002

William Storrar, *Scottish Identity: A Christian Vision*, Handsel Press, 1990

General

Neal Ascherson, *Stone Voices: The Search for Scotland*, Granta Books, 2002

Walter Bower and D. E. R. Watt (ed), *A History Book for Scots*, Mercat Press, 1998

T. M. Devine, *The Scottish Nation 1700–2000*, Penguin Books, 1999

Gordon Donaldson, *Scottish Historical Documents*, Neil Wilson Publishing, 1974

Christopher Harvie, *Scotland: A Short History*, Oxford University Press, 2002

Michael Lynch, *Scotland: A New History*, Pimlico, 1991

Louise Yeoman, *Reportage Scotland: History in the Making*, Luath Press, 2000

THE SCOTS CONFESSION OF FAITH

THE

CONFESSION

OF THE

Faith and Doctrine,

Belevit and professit be the

PROTESTANTIS OF SCOTLAND,

Exhibit to the Estaitis of the same in Parliament, and be their publick Votis authorisit, as a Doctrine groundit upon the infallibil Worde of God, *Aug.* 1560. And afterwards stablished and publicklie confirmed be sundrie Acts of Parliaments, and of lawful General Assemblies.

THE

CONFESSION

OF THE

Faith and Doctrine,

Believed and professed by the

PROTESTANTS OF SCOTLAND,

Exhibited to the Estates of Scotland in Parliament in August 1560 and approved by their public vote as doctrine founded upon the infallible Word of God, and afterwards established and publicly confirmed by various Acts of Parliament and of lawful General Assemblies.

St Matthew 24 v 14
And this glad tidings of the Kingdom shall be preached through the whole world for a witness to all nations; and then shall the end come.

A MODERN TRANSLATION
by
James Bulloch

THE PREFACE

The Estaitis of *Scotland* with the inhabitants of the same professand *Christ Jesus* his haly Evangel, to their natural Countrymen, and unto all uther realmes professand the same Lord *Jesus* with them, wish Grace, Mercie and Peace fra God the Father of our *Lord Jesus* Christ, with the Spirit of richteous Judgement, for Salvatioun.

THE PREFACE

The Estates of Scotland, with the inhabitants of Scotland who profess the holy Evangel of Jesus Christ, to their fellow countrymen and to all other nations who confess the Lord Jesus with them, wish grace, mercy, and peace from God the Father of our Lord Jesus Christ, with the Spirit of righteous judgment, for salvation.

Lang have we thristed, dear Brethren, to have notified to the Warld the Sum of that Doctrine quhilk we professe, and for the quhilk we have susteined Infamie and Danger: Bot sik hes bene the Rage of Sathan againis us, and againis *Christ Jesus* his eternal Veritie latlie now againe born amangst us, that to this daie na Time hes been graunted unto us to cleir our Consciences, as maist gladlie we wald have done. For how we have been tossit heirtofoir, the maist part of *Europe*, as we suppose, dois understand.

But seing that of the infinit Gudnes of our God (quha never sufferis his afflickit utterlie to be confoundit) abone Expectation we have obteined sum Rest and Libertie, we culd not bot set furth this brefe and plaine Confessioun of sik Doctrine as is proponed unto us, and as we beleeve and professe; partlie for Satisfactioun of our Brethren quhais hartis, we nathing doubt, have been and zit ar woundit be the despichtful rayling of sik as zit have not learned to speke well: And partlie for stapping the mouthis of impudent blasphemers, quha bauldlie damne that quhilk they have nouther heard nor zit understude.

Not that we judge that the cankred malice of sik is abill to be cured be this our simple confession; na, we knaw that the sweet savoure of the evangel is and sal be deathe unto the sonnes of perditioun. Bot we have chief respect to our weak and infirme brethren, to quham we wald communicate the bottom of our hartes, leist that they be troubled or carried awaie be diversity of rumoris, quhilk Sathan spredis against us to the defeating of this our maist godlic interprize: Protestand that gif onie man will note in this our confessioun onie Artickle or sentence repugnand to Gods halie word, that it wald pleis him of his gentleness and for christian charities sake to admonish us of the same in writing; and we upon our honoures and fidelitie, be Gods grace do promise unto him satisfactioun fra the mouth of God, that is, fra his haly scriptures, or else reformation of that quhilk he sal prove to be amisse. For God we take to recorde in our consciences, that fra our heartis we abhorre all sectis of heresie and all teachers of erronious doctrine: and that with all humilitie, we imbrace the purity of *Christs* Gospell, quhilk is the onelie fude of our sauls, and therefoir sa precious unto us, that we ar determined to suffer the extremest of warldlie daunger, rather than that we will suffer our selves to be defraudit of the sam. For heirof we ar maist certainlie perswadit, that quhasumever denieis Christ Jesus, or is aschamit of him in the presence of men, sal be denyit befoir the Father, and befoir his haly Angels. And therefoir be the assistance of the michtie Spirit of the same our Lord Jesus Christ, we firmelie purpose to abide to the end in the confessioun of this our faith, as be Artickles followis.

Long have we thirsted, dear brethren, to have made known to the world the doctrine which we profess and for which we have suffered abuse and danger; but such has been the rage of Satan against us, and against the eternal truth of Christ now recently reborn among us, that until this day we have had neither time nor opportunity to set forth our faith, as gladly we would have done. For how we have been afflicted until now the greater part of Europe, we suppose, knows well.

But since by the infinite goodness of our God (who never suffers His afflicted to be utterly confounded) we have received unexpected rest and liberty, we could not do other than set forth this brief and plain Confession of that doctrine which is set before us, and which we believe and confess; partly to satisfy our brethren whose hearts, we suspect, have been and are grieved by the slanders against us; and partly to silence impudent blasphemers who boldly condemn that which they have not heard and do not understand.

We do not suppose that such malice can be cured merely by our Confession, for we know that the sweet savour of the Gospel is, and shall be, death to the sons of perdition; but we are considering chiefly our own weaker brethren, to whom we would communicate our deepest thoughts, lest they be troubled or carried away by the different rumours which Satan spreads against us to defeat our godly enterprise, protesting that if any man will note in our Confession any chapter or sentence contrary to God's Holy Word, that it would please him of his gentleness and for Christian charity's sake to inform us of it in writing; and we, upon our honour, do promise him that by God's grace we shall give him satisfaction from the mouth of God, that is, from Holy Scripture, or else we shall alter whatever he can prove to be wrong. For we call on God to record that from our hearts we abhor all heretical sects and all teachers of false doctrine, and that with all humility we embrace the purity of Christ's Gospel, which is the one food of our souls and therefore so precious to us that we are determined to suffer the greatest of worldly dangers, rather than let our souls be defrauded of it. For we are completely convinced that whoever denies Christ Jesus, or is ashamed of Him in the presence of men, shall be denied before the Father and before His holy angels. Therefore by the aid of the mighty Spirit of our Lord Jesus Christ we firmly intend to endure to the end in the confession of our faith, as in the following chapters.

Article I

OF GOD

We confesse and acknowledge ane onelie God, to whom only we must cleave, whom onelie we must serve, whom onelie we must worship, and in whom onelie we must put our trust. Who is Eternall, Infinit, Unmeasurable, Incomprehensible, Omnipotent, Invisible: ane in

Chapter I

GOD

We confess and acknowledge one God alone, to whom alone we must cleave, whom alone we must serve, whom only we must worship, and in whom alone we put our trust. Who is eternal, infinite, immeasurable, incomprehensible, omnipotent, invisible; one in substance, and zit distinct in thre personnis, the Father, the Sone, and the holie Gost. Be whom we confesse and beleve all thingis in hevin and eirth aswel Visible as Invisible, to have been created, to be reteined in their being, and to be ruled and guyded be his inscrutable Providence, to sik end, as his Eternall Wisdome, Gudnes, and Justice hes appoynted them, to the manifestatioun of his awin glorie.

substance and yet distinct in three persons, the Father, the Son, and the Holy Ghost. By whom we confess and believe all things in heaven and earth, visible and invisible, to have been created, to be retained in their being, and to be ruled and guided by His inscrutable providence for such end as His eternal wisdom, goodness, and justice have appointed, and to the manifestation of His own glory.

ARTICLE II
OF THE CREATIOUN OF MAN

We confesse and acknawledge this our GOD to have created man, to wit, our first father *Adam*, to his awin image and similitude, to whome he gave wisdome, lordship, justice, free-wil, and cleir knawledge of himselfe, sa that in the haill nature of man there culd be noted no imperfectioun. Fra quhilk honour and perfectioun, man and woman did bothe fal: the woman being deceived be the Serpent, and man obeying the voyce of the woman, both conspyring against the Soveraigne Majestie of GOD, who in expressed words had before threatned deith, gif they presumed to eit of the forbidden tre.

CHAPTER II
THE CREATION OF MAN

We confess and acknowledge that our God has created man, i.e., our first father, Adam, after His own image and likeness, to whom He gave wisdom, lordship, justice, free will, and self-consciousness, so that in the whole nature of man no imperfection could be found. From this dignity and perfection man and woman both fell; the woman being deceived by the serpent and man obeying the voice of the woman, both conspiring against the sovereign majesty of God, who in clear words had previously threatened death if they presumed to eat of the forbidden tree.

ARTICLE III
OF ORIGINAL SINNE

Be quhilk transgressioun, commonlie called Original sinne, wes the Image of GOD utterlie defaced in man, and he and his posteritie of nature become enimies to GOD, slaves to Sathan, and servandis unto sin. In samekle that deith everlasting hes had, and sall have power and dominioun over all that have not been, ar not, or sal not be regenerate from above: quhilk regeneratioun is wrocht be the power of the holie Gost, working in the hartes of the elect of GOD, ane assured faith in the promise of GOD, reveiled to us in his word, be quhilk faith we apprehend Christ Jesus, with the graces and benefites promised in him.

CHAPTER III
ORIGINAL SIN

By this transgression, generally known as original sin, the image of God was utterly defaced in man, and he and his children became by nature hostile to God, slaves to Satan, and servants to sin. And thus everlasting death has had, and shall have, power and dominion over all who have not been, are not, or shall not be reborn from above. This rebirth is wrought by the power of the Holy Ghost creating in the hearts of God's chosen ones an assured faith in the promise of God revealed to us in His Word; by this faith we grasp Christ Jesus with the graces and blessings promised in Him.

ARTICLE IV
OF THE REVELATIOUN OF THE PROMISE

For this we constantlie beleeve, that GOD, after the feirfull and horrible defectioun of man fra his obedience, did seek *Adam* againe, call upon him, rebuke his sinne, convict him of the same, and in the end made unto him ane most joyful promise, to wit, *That the seed of the woman suld break down the serpents head*, that is, he suld destroy the works of the Devill. Quhilk promise, as it was repeated, and made mair cleare from time to time; so was it imbraced with joy, and maist constantlie received of al the faithfull, from *Adam* to *Noe*, from *Noe* to *Abraham*, from *Abraham* to *David*, and so furth to the incarnatioun of *Christ Jesus*, all (we meane the faithfull Fathers under the Law) did see the joyfull daie of *Christ Jesus*, and did rejoyce.

CHAPTER IV
THE REVELATION OF THE PROMISE

We constantly believe that God, after the fearful and horrible departure of man from His obedience, did seek Adam again, call upon him, rebuke and convict him of his sin, and in the end made unto him a most joyful promise, that 'the seed of the woman should bruise the head of the serpent', that is, that he should destroy the works of the devil. This promise was repeated and made clearer from time to time; it was embraced with joy, and most constantly received by all the faithful from Adam to Noah, from Noah to Abraham, from Abraham to David, and so onwards to the incarnation of Christ Jesus; all (we mean the believing fathers under the law) did see the joyful day of Christ Jesus, and did rejoice.

ARTICLE V

OF THE CONTINUANCE, INCREASE,
AND PRESERVATION OF THE KIRK

We maist constantly beleeve, that God preserved, instructed, multiplied, honoured, decored, and from death called to life, his Kirk in all ages fra *Adam*, till the cumining of *Christ Jesus* in the flesh. For *Abraham* he called from his Fathers cuntry, him he instructed, his seede he multiplied; the same he marveilouslie preserved, and mair marveilouslie delivered from the bondage and tyrannie of *Pharaoh*; to them he gave his lawes, constitutions and ceremonies; them he possessed in the land of *Canaan*; to them after Judges, and after *Saul*, he gave *David* to be king, to whome hee made promise, that of the fruite of his loynes suld ane sit for ever upon his regall seat. To this same people from time to time he sent prophets, to reduce them to the right way of their God: from the quhilk oftentimes they declined be idolatry. And albeit that for their stubborne contempt of Justice, he was compelled to give them in the hands of their enimies, as befoir was threatned be the mouth of *Moses*, in sa meikle that the haly cittie was destroyed, the temple burnt with fire, and the haill land left desolate the space of lxx years: zit of mercy did he reduce them againe to *Jerusalem*, where the cittie and temple were reedified, and they against all temptations and assaultes of Sathan did abide, till the *Messias* come, according to the promise.

ARTICLE VI

OF THE INCARNATION OF CHRIST JESUS

Quhen the fulnes of time came, God sent his Sonne, his eternall Wisdome, the substance of his awin glory in this warld, quha tuke the nature of man-head of the substance of woman, to wit, of a virgine, and that be operatioun of the holie Ghost: and so was borne the just seede of *David*, the Angell of the great counsell of God, the very *Messias* promised, whome we confesse and acknawledge *Emmanuel*, very God and very man, two perfit natures united, and joyned in one persoun. Be quhilk our Confessioun we condemne the damnable and pestilent heresies of *Arius, Marcion, Eutyches, Nestorius*, and sik uthers, as either did denie the eternitie of his God-head, or the veritie of his humaine nature, or confounded them, or zit devided them.

ARTICLE VII

WHY IT BEHOOVED THE MEDIATOR TO BE VERY GOD
AND VERY MAN

We acknawledge and confesse, that this maist wonderous conjunction betwixt the God-head and the man-head in *Christ Jesus*, did proceed from the eternall and immutable decree of GOD, from quhilk al our salvatioun springs and depends.

CHAPTER V

THE CONTINUANCE, INCREASE, AND
PRESERVATION OF THE KIRK

We most surely believe that God preserved, instructed, multiplied, honoured, adorned, and called from death to life His Kirk in all ages since Adam until the coming of Christ Jesus in the flesh. For He called Abraham from his father's country, instructed him, and multiplied his seed; he marvellously preserved him, and more marvellously delivered his seed from the bondage and tyranny of Pharaoh; to them He gave His laws, constitutions, and ceremonies; to them He gave the land of Canaan; after He had given them judges, and afterwards Saul, He gave David to be king, to whom He gave promise that of the fruit of his loins should one sit forever upon his royal throne. To this same people from time to time He sent prophets, to recall them to the right way of their God, from which sometimes they strayed by idolatry. And although, because of their stubborn contempt for righteousness He was compelled to give them into the hands of their enemies, as had previously been threatened by the mouth of Moses, so that the holy city was destroyed, the temple burned with fire, and the whole land desolate for seventy years, yet in mercy He restored them again to Jerusalem, where the city and temple were rebuilt, and they endured against all temptations and assaults of Satan till the Messiah came according to the promise.

CHAPTER VI

THE INCARNATION OF CHRIST JESUS

When the fullness of time came God sent His Son, His eternal Wisdom, the substance of His own glory, into this world, who took the nature of humanity from the substance of a woman, a virgin, by means of the Holy Ghost. And so was born the 'just seed of David', the 'Angel of the great counsel of God', the very Messiah promised, whom we confess and acknowledge to be Emmanuel, true God and true man, two perfect natures united and joined in one person. So by our Confession we condemn the damnable and pestilent heresies of Arius, Marcion, Eutyches, Nestorius, and such others as did either deny the eternity of His Godhead, or the truth of His humanity, or confounded them, or else divided them.

CHAPTER VII

WHY THE MEDIATOR HAD TO BE TRUE GOD
AND TRUE MAN

We acknowledge and confess that this wonderful union between the Godhead and the humanity in Christ Jesus did arise from the eternal and immutable decree of God from which all our salvation springs and depends.

ARTICLE VIII

OF ELECTION

For that same eternall God and Father, who of meere grace elected us in *Christ Jesus* his Sonne, befoir the foundatioun of the warld was laide, appointed him to be our Head, our Brother, our Pastor, and great Bischop of our sauls. Bot because that the enimitie betwixt the justice of God and our sins was sik, that na flesh be it selfe culd or might have attained unto God: It behooved that the Sonne of God suld descend unto us, and tak himselfe a bodie of our bodie, flesh of our flesh, and bone of our bones, and so become the Mediator betwixt God and man, giving power to so many as beleeve in him, to be the sonnes of God; as himselfe dois witnesse, *I passe up to my Father, and unto zour Father, to my God, and unto zour God*. Be quhilk maist holie fraternitie, quhatsaever wee have tynt in *Adam*, is restored unto us agayne. And for this cause, ar we not affrayed to cal God our Father, not sa meikle because he hes created us, quhilk we have common with the reprobate; as for that, that he hes given to us his onely Sonne, to be our brother, and given to us grace, to acknawledge and imbrace him for our onlie Mediatour, as before is said. It behooved farther the Messias and Redemer to be very God and very man, because he was to underlie the punischment due for our transgressiouns, and to present himselfe in the presence of his Fathers Judgment, as in our persone, to suffer for our transgression and inobedience, be death to overcome him that was author of death. Bot because the onely God-head culd not suffer death, neither zit culd the onlie man-head overcome the samin, he joyned both togither in one persone, that the imbecillitie of the ane, suld suffer and be subject to death, quhilk we had deserved: And the infinit and invincible power of the uther, to wit, of the God-head, suld triumph and purchesse to us life, libertie, and perpetuall victory: And so we confes, and maist undoubtedly beleeve.

ARTICLE IX

OF CHRIST'S DEATH, PASSION, AND BURIAL

That our Lord *Jesus* offered himselfe a voluntary Sacrifice unto his Father for us, that he suffered contradiction of sinners, that he was wounded and plagued for our transgressiouns, that hee being the cleane innocent Lambe of God, was damned in the presence of an earthlie judge, that we suld be absolved befoir the tribunal seat of our God. That he suffered not onlie the cruell death of the Crosse, quhilk was accursed be the sentence of God; bot also that he suffered for a season the wrath of his Father, quhilk sinners had deserved. Bot zit we avow that he remained the only welbeloved and blessed Sonne of his Father, even in the middest of his anguish and torment, quhilk hee suffered in bodie and saule, to mak the full satisfaction for the sinnes of the people. After the quhilk we confesse and avow, that there remaines na uther Sacrifice for sinne, quhilk gif ony affirme, we nathing dout to avow that they ar blasphemous against *Christs* death, and the everlasting purgatioun and satisfactioun purchased to us be the same.

CHAPTER VIII

ELECTION

That same eternal God and Father, who by grace alone chose us in His Son Christ Jesus before the foundation of the world was laid, appointed Him to be our head, our brother, our pastor, and the great bishop of our souls. But since the opposition between the justice of God and our sins was such that no flesh by itself could or might have attained unto God, it behoved the Son of God to descend unto us and take Himself a body of our body, flesh of our flesh, and bone of our bone, and so become the Mediator between God and man, giving power to as many as believe in Him to be the sons of God; as He Himself says, 'I ascend to My Father and to your Father, to My God and to your God'. By this most holy brotherhood whatever we have lost in Adam is restored to us again. Therefore we are not afraid to call God our Father, not so much because He has created us, which we have in common with the reprobate, as because He has given unto us His only Son to be our brother, and given us grace to acknowledge and embrace Him as our only Mediator. Further, it behoved the Messiah and Redeemer to be true God and true man, because He was able to undergo the punishment of our transgressions and to present Himself in the presence of His Father's Judgment, as in our stead, to suffer for our transgression and disobedience, and by death to overcome him that was the author of death. But because the Godhead alone could not suffer death, and neither could manhood overcome death. He joined both together in one person, that the weakness of one should suffer and be subject to death – which we had deserved – and the infinite and invincible power of the other, that is, of the Godhead, should triumph, and purchase for us life, liberty, and perpetual victory. So we confess, and most undoubtedly believe.

CHAPTER IX

CHRIST'S DEATH, PASSION, AND BURIAL

That our Lord Jesus offered Himself a voluntary sacrifice unto His Father for us, that He suffered contradiction of sinners, that He was wounded and plagued for our transgressions, that He, the clean innocent Lamb of God, was condemned in the presence of an earthly judge, that we should be absolved before the judgment seat of our God; that He suffered not only the cruel death of the cross, which was accursed by the sentence of God; but also that He suffered for a season the wrath of His Father which sinners had deserved. But yet we avow that He remained the only, well beloved, and blessed Son of His Father even in the midst of His anguish and torment which He suffered in body and soul to make full atonement for the sins of His people. From this we confess and avow that there remains no other sacrifice for sin; if any affirm so, we do not hesitate to say that they are blasphemers against Christ's death and the everlasting atonement thereby purchased for us.

ARTICLE X
OF THE RESURRECTION

We undoubtedlie beleeve, that in sa mekle as it wes impossible, that the dolours of death sulde reteine in bondage the Author of life, that our LORD JESUS crucified, dead and buryed, quha descended into hell, did ryse agayne for our Justificatioun, and destroying of him quha wes the Author of death, brocht life againe to us, that wer subject to death, and to the bondage of the same. We knaw that his Resurrectioun wes confirmed be the testimonie of his verie Enemies, be the resurrectioun of the dead, quhais Sepultures did oppen, and they did ryse, and appeared to mony, within the Cittie of *Jerusalem*. It wes also confirmed be the testimonie of his Angels, and be the senses and judgements of his Apostles, and of uthers, quha had conversatioun, and did eate and drink with him, after his Resurrection.

CHAPTER X
THE RESURRECTION

We undoubtedly believe, since it was impossible that the sorrows of death should retain in bondage the Author of life, that our Lord Jesus crucified, dead, and buried, who descended into hell, did rise again for our justification, and the destruction of him who was the author of death, and brought life again to us who were subject to death and its bondage. We know that His resurrection was confirmed by the testimony of His enemies, and by the resurrection of the dead, whose sepulchres did open, and they did rise and appear to many within the city of Jerusalem. It was also confirmed by the testimony of His angels, and by the senses and judgment of His apostles and of others, who had conversation, and did eat and drink with Him after His resurrection.

ARTICLE XI
OF THE ASCENSION

We nathing doubt, bot the self same bodie, quhilk was borne of the Virgine, was crucified, dead, and buried, and quhilk did rise againe, did ascend into the heavens, for the accomplishment of all thinges: Quhere in our names, and for our comfort, he hes received all power in heaven and eirth, quhere he sittes at the richt hand of the Father, inaugurate in his kingdome, Advocate and onlie Mediator for us. Quhilk glorie, honour, and prerogative, he alone amonges the brethren sal possess, till that all his Enimies be made his futestule, as that we undoubtedlie beleeve they sall be in the finall Judgment: To the Execution whereof we certainelie believe, that the same our Lord JESUS sall visiblie returne, as that hee was sene to ascend. And then we firmely beleve, that the time of refreshing and restitutioun of all things sall cum, in samekle that thir, that fra the beginning have suffered violence, injurie, and wrang, for richteousnes sake, sal inherit that blessed immortalitie promised fra the beginning.

Bot contrariwise the stubburne, inobedient, cruell oppressours, filthie personis, idolaters, and all such sortes of unfaithfull, sal be cast in the dungeoun of utter darkenesse, where their worme sall not die, nether zit their fyre sall bee extinguished. The remembrance of quhilk day, and of the Judgement to be executed in the same, is not onelie to us ane brydle, whereby our carnal lustes are refrained, bot alswa sik inestimable comfort, that nether may the threatning of worldly Princes, nether zit the feare of temporal death and present danger, move us to renounce and forsake that blessed societie, quhilk we the members have with our Head and onelie Mediator CHRIST JESUS: Whom we confesse and avow to be the Messias promised, the onlie Head of his Kirk, our just Lawgiver, our onlie hie Priest, Advocate, and Mediator. In quhilk honoures and offices, gif man or Angell presume to intruse themself, we utterlie detest and abhorre them, as blasphemous to our Soveraigne and supreme Governour CHRIST JESUS.

CHAPTER XI
THE ASCENSION

We do not doubt but that the selfsame body which was born of the virgin, was crucified, dead, and buried, and which did rise again, did ascend into the heavens, for the accomplishment of all things, where in our name and for our comfort He has received all power in heaven and earth, where He sits at the right hand of the Father, having received His kingdom, the only advocate and mediator for us. Which glory, honour, and prerogative, He alone amongst the brethren shall possess till all His enemies are made His footstool, as we undoubtedly believe they shall be in the Last Judgment. We believe that the same Lord Jesus shall visibly return for this Last judgment as He was seen to ascend. And then, we firmly believe, the time of refreshing and restitution of all things shall come, so that those who from the beginning have suffered violence, injury, and wrong, for righteousness' sake, shall inherit that blessed immortality promised them from the beginning. But, on the other hand, the stubborn, disobedient, cruel persecutors, filthy persons, idolators, and all sorts of the unbelieving, shall be cast into the dungeon of utter darkness, where their worm shall not die, nor their fire be quenched. The remembrance of that day, and of the Judgment to be executed in it, is not only a bridle by which our carnal lusts are restrained but also such inestimable comfort that neither the threatening of worldly princes, nor the fear of present danger or of temporal death, may move us to renounce and forsake that blessed society which we, the members, have with our Head and only Mediator, Christ Jesus: whom we confess and avow to be the promised Messiah, the only Head of His Kirk, our just Lawgiver, our only High Priest, Advocate, and Mediator. To which honours and offices, if man or angel presume to intrude themselves, we utterly detest and abhor them, as blasphemous to our sovereign and supreme Governor, Christ Jesus.

ARTICLE XII

OF FAITH IN THE HOLY GOSTE

This our Faith and the assurance of the same, proceeds not fra flesh and blude, that is to say, fra na natural poweris within us, bot is the inspiration of the holy Gost: Whome we confesse GOD equall with the Father and with his Sonne, quha sanctifyis us, and bringis us in al veritie be his awin operation, without whome we sulde remaine for ever enimies to God, and ignorant of his Sonne *Christ Jesus*; for of nature we are so dead, so blind, and so perverse, that nether can we feill when we are pricked, see the licht when it shines, nor assent to the will of God when it is reveiled, unles the Spirit of the Lord *Jesus* quicken that quhilk is dead, remove the darknesse from our myndes, and bowe our stubburne hearts to the obedience of his blessed will. And so as we confesse, that God the Father created us, when we were not, as his Sonne our Lord *Jesus* redeemed us, when wee were enimies to him; so also do we confesse that the holy Gost doth sanctifie and regenerat us, without all respect of ony merite proceeding from us, be it before, or be it after our Regeneration. To speak this ane thing zit in mair plaine words: As we willingly spoyle our selves of all honour and gloir of our awin Creation and Redemption, so do we also of our Regeneration and Sanctification, for of our selves we ar not sufficient to think one gude thocht, bot he quha hes begun the wark in us, is onlie he that continewis us in the same, to the praise and glorie of his undeserved grace.

CHAPTER XII

FAITH IN HOLY GHOST

Our faith and its assurance do not proceed from flesh and blood, that is to say, from natural powers within us, but are the inspiration of the Holy Ghost; whom we confess to be God, equal with the Father and with His Son, who sanctifies us, and brings us into all truth by His own working, without whom we should remain forever enemies to God and ignorant of His Son, Christ Jesus. For by nature we are so dead, blind, and perverse, that neither can we feel when we are pricked, see the light when it shines, nor assent to the will of God when it is revealed, unless the Spirit of the Lord Jesus quicken that which is dead, remove the darkness from our minds, and bow our stubborn hearts to the obedience of His blessed will. And so, as we confess that God the Father created us when we were not, as His Son our Lord Jesus redeemed us when we were enemies to Him, so also do we confess that the Holy Ghost does sanctify and regenerate us, without respect to any merit proceeding from us, be it before or be it after our regeneration. To put this even more plainly; as we willingly disclaim any honour and glory for our own creation and redemption, so do we willingly also for our regeneration and sanctification; for by ourselves we are not capable of thinking one good thought, but He who has begun the work in us alone continues us in it, to the praise and glory of His undeserved grace.

ARTICLE XIII

OF THE CAUSE OF GUDE WARKIS

Sa that the cause of gude warkis, we confesse to be not our free wil, bot the Spirit of the Lord *Jesus*, who dwelling in our hearts be trewe faith, bringis furth sik warkis, as God hes prepared for us to walke in. For this wee maist boldelie affirme, that blasphemy it is to say, that *Christ* abydes in the heartes of sik, as in whome there is no spirite of sanctification. And therefore we feir not to affirme, that murtherers, oppressers, cruell persecuters, adulterers, huremongers, filthy persouns, Idolaters, drunkards, thieves, and al workers of iniquity, have nether trew faith, nether ony portion of the Spirit of the Lord JESUS, so long as obstinatlie they continew in their wickednes. For how soone that ever the Spirit of the Lord JESUS, quhilk Gods elect children receive be trew faith, taks possession in the heart of ony man, so soone dois he regenerate and renew the same man. So that he beginnis to hait that quhilk before he loved, and begins to love that quhilk befoir he hated; and fra thine cummis that continuall battell, quhilk is betwixt the flesh and the Spirit in Gods children, till the flesh and natural man, according to the awin corruption, lustes for things pleisand and delectable unto the self, and grudges in adversity, is lyfted up in prosperity, and at every moment is prone and reddie to offend the majestie of God. Bot the spirite of God, quhilk gives witnessing to our spirite, that we are the sonnes of God, makis us to resist filthie

CHAPTER XIII

THE CAUSE OF GOOD WORKS

The cause of good works, we confess, is not our free will, but the Spirit of the Lord Jesus, who dwells in our hearts by true faith, brings forth such works as God has prepared for us to walk in. For we most boldly affirm that it is blasphemy to say that Christ abides in the hearts of those in whom is no spirit of sanctification. Therefore we do not hesitate to affirm that murderers, oppressors, cruel persecutors, adulterers, filthy persons, idolators, drunkards, thieves, and all workers of iniquity, have neither true faith nor anything of the Spirit of the Lord Jesus, so long as they obstinately continue in wickedness. For as soon as the Spirit of the Lord Jesus, whom God's chosen children receive by true faith, takes possession of the heart of any man, so soon does He regenerate and renew him, so that he begins to hate what before he loved, and to love what he hated before. Thence comes that continual battle which is between the flesh and the Spirit in God's children, while the flesh and the natural man, being corrupt, lust for things pleasant and delightful to themselves, are envious in adversity and proud in prosperity, and every moment prone and ready to offend the majesty of God. But the Spirit of God, who bears witness to our spirit that we are the sons of God, makes us resist filthy pleasures and groan in God's presence for deliverance from this bondage of corruption, and finally to triumph over sin so that it does not reign in our mortal

plesures, and to groane in Gods presence, for deliverance fra this bondage of corruption; and finally to triumph over sin, that it reygne not in our mortal bodyis. This battell hes not the carnal men, being destitute of Gods Spirite, bot dois followe and obey sinne with greedines, and without repentance, even as the Devill, and their corrupt lustes do prick them. Bot the sonnes of God, as before wes said, dois fecht against sinne; dois sob and murne, when they perceive themselves tempted in iniquitie; and gif they fal, they rise againe with earnest and unfained repentance: And thir thingis they do not be their awin power, bot be the power of the Lord *Jesus*, without whom they were able to do nothing.

bodies. Other men do not share this conflict since they do not have God's Spirit, but they readily follow and obey sin and feel no regrets, since they act as the devil and their corrupt nature urge. But the sons of God fight against sin; sob and mourn when they find themselves tempted to do evil; and, if they fall, rise again with earnest and unfeigned repentance. They do these things, not by their own power, but by the power of the Lord Jesus, apart from whom they can do nothing.

Article XIV
WHAT WARKIS ARE REPUTIT GUDE BEFOIR GOD

We confesse and acknawledge, that God hes given to man his holy Law, in quhilk not only ar forbidden all sik warkes as displeis and offend his godly Majestie, but alswa ar commanded al sik as pleis him, and as hes promised to reward. And thir warkes be of twa sortes. The ane are done to the honour of God, the uther to the profite of our Nichtbouris; and both have the reveiled will of God for their assurance. To have ane God, to worship and honour him, to call upon him in all our troubles, reverence his holy name, to heare his word, to beleve the same, to communicate with his holy Sacraments, are the warkes of the first Tabill. To honour Father, Mother, Princes, Rulers, and superiour powers; to love them, to support them, zea to obey their charges (not repugning to the commaundment of God), to save the lives of innocents, to represse tyrannie, to defend the oppressed, to keepe our bodies cleane and halie, to live in sobernes and temperance, to deall justlie with all men both in word and deed; and finally, to represse all appetite of our Nichbouris hurt, are the gude warkes of the secund Tabill, quhilk are maist pleising and acceptabill unto God, as thir warkes that are commanded be himselfe. The contrary quhairof is sinne maist odious, quhilk alwayes displeisis him, and provokes him to anger: As not to call upon him alone, when we have need; not to heare his word with reverence, to contemne and despise it; to have or worship idols, to maintene and defend Idolatrie; lichthe to esteeme the reverend name of God; to prophane, abuse, or contemne the Sacraments of *Christ Jesus*; to disobey or resist ony that God lies placed in authoritie (quhil they passe not over the bounds of their office); to murther, or to consent thereto, to beare hatred, or to let innocent blude bee sched, gif wee may withstand it. And finally, the transgression of ony uther commandement in the first or secund Tabill, we confesse and affirme to be sinne, by the quhilk Gods anger and displesure is kindled against the proud unthankfull warld. So that gude warkes we affirme to be thir onlie, that are done in faith, and at God commandment, quha in his Lawe hes expressed what the thingis be that pleis him. And evill warkis we affirme not only thir that expressedly ar done against Gods commaundement: bot thir alswa

Chapter XIV
THE WORKS WHICH ARE COUNTED GOOD BEFORE GOD

We confess and acknowledge that God has given to man His holy law, in which not only all such works as displease and offend His godly majesty are forbidden, but also those which please Him and which He has promised to reward are commanded. These works are of two kinds. The one is done to the honour of God, the other to the profit of our neighbour, and both have the revealed will of God as their assurance. To have one God, to worship and honour Him, to call upon Him in all our troubles, to reverence His holy Name, to hear His Word and to believe it, and to share in His holy sacraments, belong to the first kind. To honour father, mother, princes, rulers, and superior powers; to love them, to support them, to obey their orders if they are not contrary to the commands of God, to save the lives of the innocent, to repress tyranny, to defend the oppressed, to keep our bodies clean and holy, to live in soberness and temperance, to deal justly with all men in word and deed, and, finally, to repress any desire to harm our neighbour, are the good works of the second kind, and these are most pleasing and acceptable to God as He has commanded them Himself. Acts to the contrary are sins, which always displease Him and provoke Him to anger, such as, not to call upon Him alone when we have need, not to hear His Word with reverence, but to condemn and despise it, to have or worship idols, to maintain and defend idolatry, lightly to esteem the reverend name of God, to profane, abuse, or condemn the sacraments of Christ Jesus, to disobey or resist any whom God has placed in authority, so long as they do not exceed the bounds of their office, to murder, or to consent thereto, to bear hatred, or to let innocent blood be shed if we can prevent it. In conclusion, we confess and affirm that the breach of any other commandment of the first or second kind is sin, by which God's anger and displeasure are kindled against the proud, unthankful world. So that we affirm good works to be those alone which are done in faith and at the command of God who, in His law, has set forth the things that please Him. We affirm that evil works are not only those expressly done against God's command, but also, in religious matters and the worship of God, those things which have no other warrant than the invention and opinion of man.

that in matteris of Religioun, and worschipping of God, hes na uther assurance bot the inventioun, and opinioun of man: quhilk God fra the beginning hes ever rejected, as be the Prophet *Esay*, and be our Maister CHRIST JESUS we ar taught in thir words, *In vaine do they worschip me, teaching the doctrines the precepts of men.*

From the beginning God has rejected such, as we learn from the words of the prophet Isaiah and of our master, Christ Jesus, 'In vain do they worship Me, teaching the doctrines and commandments of men.'

ARTICLE XV
OF THE PERFECTIOUN OF THE LAW,
AND THE IMPERFECTIOUN OF MAN

The Law of God we confesse and acknawledge maist just, maist equall, maist halie, and maist perfite, commaunding thir thingis, quhilk being wrocht in perfectioun, were abill to give life, and abill to bring man to eternall felicitie. Bot our nature is sa corrupt, sa weake, and sa unperfite, that we ar never abill to fulfill the warkes of the Law in perfectioun. Zea, gif we say we have na sinne, evin after we are regenerate, we deceive our selves, and the veritie of God is not in us. And therefore, it behovis us to apprehend *Christ Jesus* with his justice and satisfaction, quha is the end and accomplishment of the Law, be quhome we ar set at this liberty, that the curse and malediction of God fall not upon us, albeit we fulfill not the same in al pointes. For God the Father beholding us, in the body of his Sonne *Christ Jesus*, acceptis our imperfite obedience, as it were perfite, and covers our warks, quhilk ar defyled with mony spots, with the justice of his Sonne. We do not meane that we ar so set at liberty, that we awe na obedience to the Law (for that before wee have plainly confessed), bot this we affirme, that na man in eird (*Christ Jesus* onlie except) hes given, gives, or sall give in worke, that obedience to the Law, quhilk the Law requiris. Bot when we have done all things, we must falle down and unfeinedly confesse, that we are unprofitable servands. And therefore, quhosoever boastis themselves of the merits of their awin works, or put their trust in the works of Supererogation, boast themselves in that quhilk is nocht, and put their trust in damnable Idolatry.

CHAPTER XV
THE PERFECTION OF THE LAW
AND THE IMPERFECTION OF MAN

We confess and acknowledge that the law of God is most just, equal, holy, and perfect, commanding those things which, when perfectly done, can give life and bring man to eternal felicity; but our nature is so corrupt, weak, and imperfect, that we are never able perfectly to fulfil the works of the law. Even after we are reborn, if we say that we have no sin, we deceive ourselves and the truth of God is not in us. It is therefore essential for us to lay hold on Christ Jesus, in His righteousness and His atonement, since He is the end and consummation of the Law and since it is by Him that we are set at liberty so that the curse of God may not fall upon us, even though we do not fulfil the Law in all points. For as God the Father beholds us in the body of His Son Christ Jesus, He accepts our imperfect obedience as if it were perfect, and covers our works, which are defiled with many stains, with the righteousness of His Son. We do not mean that we are so set at liberty that we owe no obedience to the Law – for we have already acknowledged its place – but we affirm that no man on earth, with the sole exception of Christ Jesus, has given, gives, or shall give in action that obedience to the Law which the Law requires. When we have done all things we must fall down and unfeignedly confess that we are unprofitable servants. Therefore, whoever boasts of the merits of his own works or puts his trust in works of supererogation, boasts of what does not exist, and puts his trust in damnable idolatry.

ARTICLE XVI
OF THE KIRK

As we beleve in ane God, Father, Sonne, and haly Ghaist; sa do we maist constantly beleeve, that from the beginning there hes bene, and now is, and to the end of the warld sall be, ane Kirk, that is to say, ane company and multitude of men chosen of God, who richtly worship and imbrace him be trew faith in *Christ Jesus*, quha is the only head of the same Kirk, quhilk alswa is the bodie and spouse of *Christ Jesus*, quhilk Kirk is catholike, that is, universal, because it conteinis the Elect of all ages, of all realmes, nations, and tongues, be they of the *Jewes*, or be they of the Gentiles, quha have communion and societie with God the Father, and with his Son *Christ Jesus*, throw the sanctification of his haly Spirit: and therefore it is called the communioun, not of prophane persoues, bot of Saincts, quha as citizenis of the heavenly *Jerusalem*,

CHAPTER XVI
THE KIRK

As we believe in one God, Father, Son, and Holy Ghost, so we firmly believe that from the beginning there has been, now is, and to the end of the world shall be, one Kirk, that is to say, one company and multitude of men chosen by God, who rightly worship and embrace Him by true faith in Christ Jesus, who is the only Head of the Kirk, even as it is the body and spouse of Christ Jesus. This Kirk is Catholic, that is, universal, because it contains the chosen of all ages, of all realms, nations, and tongues, be they of the Jews or be they of the Gentiles, who have communion and society with God the Father, and with His Son, Christ Jesus, through the sanctification of His Holy Spirit. It is therefore called the communion, not of profane persons, but of saints, who, as citizens of the heavenly Jerusalem, have the fruit of inestimable benefits, one God, one Lord Jesus, one faith, and one baptism.

have the fruitioun of the maist inestimable benefites, to wit, of ane God, ane Lord *Jesus*, ane faith, and ane baptisme: Out of the quhilk Kirk, there is nouther lyfe, nor eternall felicitie. And therefore we utterly abhorre the blasphemie of them that affirme, that men quhilk live according to equitie and justice, sal be saved, quhat Religioun that ever they have professed. For as without *Christ Jesus* there is nouther life nor salvation; so sal there nane be participant therof, bot sik as the Father hes given unto his Sonne *Christ Jesus*, and they that in time cum unto him, avowe his doctrine, and beleeve into him, we comprehend the children with the faithfull parentes. This Kirk is invisible, knawen onelie to God, quha alane knawis whome he hes chosen; and comprehends as weill (as said is) the Elect that be departed, commonlie called the *Kirk Triumphant*, and they that zit live and fecht against sinne and *Sathan* as sall live hereafter.

Out of this Kirk there is neither life nor eternal felicity. Therefore we utterly abhor the blasphemy of those who hold that men who live according to equity and justice shall be saved, no matter what religion they profess. For since there is neither life nor salvation without Christ Jesus; so shall none have part therein but those whom the Father has given unto His Son Christ Jesus, and those who in time come to Him, avow His doctrine, and believe in Him. (We include the children with the believing parents.) This Kirk is invisible, known only to God, who alone knows whom He has chosen, and includes both the chosen who are departed, the Kirk triumphant, those who yet live and fight against sin and Satan, and those who shall live hereafter.

Article XVII

OF THE IMMORTALITIE OF THE SAULES

The Elect departed are in peace and rest fra their labours: Not that they sleep, and come to a certaine oblivion, as some Phantastickes do affirme; bot that they are delivered fra all feare and torment, and all temptatioun, to quhilk we and all Goddis Elect are subject in this life, and therefore do beare the name of the *Kirk Militant*: As contrariwise, the reprobate and unfaithfull departed have anguish, torment, and paine, that cannot be expressed. Sa that nouther are the ane nor the uther in sik sleepe that they feele not joy or torment, as the Parable of *Christ Jesus* in the 16th of *Luke*, his words to the thiefe, and thir wordes of the saules crying under the Altar, *O Lord, thou that art righteous and just, How lang sall thou not revenge our blude upon thir that dwellis in the Eird?* dois testifie.

Chapter XVII

THE IMMORTALITY OF SOULS

The chosen departed are in peace, and rest from their labours; not that they sleep and are lost in oblivion as some fanatics hold, for they are delivered from all fear and torment, and all the temptations to which we and all God's chosen are subject in this life, and because of which we are called the Kirk Militant. On the other hand, the reprobate and unfaithful departed have anguish, torment, and pain which cannot be expressed. Neither the one nor the other is in such sleep that they feel no joy or torment, as is testified by Christ's parable in St Luke XVI, His words to the thief, and the words of the souls crying under the altar, 'O Lord, Thou that art righteous and just, how long shalt Thou not revenge our blood upon those that dwell in the earth?'

Article XVIII

OF THE NOTIS, BE THE QUHILK THE TREWE KIRK IS
DECERNIT FRA THE FALSE, AND QUHA SALL BE JUDGE OF
THE DOCTRINE

Because that *Sathan* from the beginning hes laboured to deck his pestilent Synagoge with the title of the Kirk of God, and hes inflamed the hertes of cruell murtherers to persecute, trouble, and molest the trewe Kirk and members thereof, as *Cain* did *Abell, Ismael Isaac, Esau Jacob*, and the haill Priesthood of the *Jewes Christ Jesus* himselfe, and his Apostles after him. It is ane thing maist requisite, that the true Kirk be decerned fra the filthie Synagogues, be cleare and perfite notes, least we being deceived, receive and imbrace, to our awin condemnation, the ane for the uther. The notes, signes, and assured takens whereby the immaculate Spouse of *Christ Jesus* is knawen fra the horrible harlot, the Kirk malignant, we affirme, are nouther Antiquitie, Title usurpit, lineal Descence, Place appointed, nor multitude of men approving ane error. For *Cain*, in age and title, was preferred to *Abel* and *Seth*: Jerusalem

Chapter XVIII

THE NOTES BY WHICH THE TRUE KIRK SHALL BE
DETERMINED FROM THE FALSE, AND WHO SHALL BE
JUDGE OF DOCTRINE

Since Satan has laboured from the beginning to adorn his pestilent synagogue with the title of the Kirk of God, and has incited cruel murderers to persecute, trouble, and molest the true Kirk and its members, as Cain did to Abel, Ishmael to Isaac, Esau to Jacob, and the whole priesthood of the Jews to Christ Jesus Himself and His apostles after Him. So it is essential that the true Kirk be distinguished from the filthy synagogues by clear and perfect notes lest we, being deceived, receive and embrace, to our own condemnation, the one for the other. The notes, signs, and assured tokens whereby the spotless bride of Christ is known from the horrible harlot, the false Kirk, we state, are neither antiquity, usurped title, lineal succession, appointed place, nor the numbers of men approving an error. For Cain was before Abel and Seth in age and title; Jerusalem had precedence above all other parts of the earth, for in it were priests lineally had prerogative above all places of the eird, where alswa were the Priests lineally descended fra *Aaron*, and greater number followed the Scribes, Pharisies, and Priestes,then unfainedly beleeved and approved *Christ Jesus* and his doctrine: And zit, as we suppose, no man of sound judgment will grant, that ony of the forenamed were the Kirk of God. The notes therefore of the trew Kirk of God we beleeve, confesse, and avow to be, first, the trew preaching of the Worde of God, into the quhilk God hes revealed himselfe unto us, as the writings of the Prophets and Apostles dois declair. Secundly, the right administration of the Sacraments of *Christ Jesus*, quhilk man be annexed unto the word and promise of God, to seale and confirme the same in our hearts. Last, Ecclesiastical discipline uprightlie ministred, as Goddis Worde prescribes, whereby vice is repressed, and vertew nurished. Wheresoever then thir former notes are scene, and of ony time continue (be the number never so fewe, about two or three), there, without all doubt, is the trew Kirk of *Christ*: Who, according unto his promise, is in the middis of them. Not that universall, of quhilk we have before spoken, bot particular, sik as wes in *Corinthus*, *Galatia*, *Ephesus*, and uther places, in quhilk the ministrie wes planted be *Paull*, and were of himselfe named the kirks of God. And sik kirks, we the inhabitantis of the Realme of *Scotland*, professoris of *Christ Jesus*, professis our selfis to have in our citties, townes, and places reformed, for the doctrine taucht in our Kirkis, conteined in the writen Worde of God, to wit, in the buiks of the Auld and New Testamentis, in those buikis we meane quhilk of the ancient have been reputed canonicall. In the quhilk we affirme, that all thingis necessary to be beleeved for the salvation of mankinde is sufficiently expressed. The interpretation quhairof, we confesse, neither appertaines to private nor publick persone, nether zit to ony Kirk, for ony preheminence or prerogative, personallie or locallie, quhilk ane hes above ane uther, bot apperteines to the Spirite of God, be the quhilk also the Scripture was written. When controversie then happines, for the right understanding of ony place or sentence of Scripture, or for the reformation of ony abuse within the Kirk of God, we ought not sa meikle to luke what men before us have said or done, as unto that quhilk the halie Ghaist uniformelie speakes within the body of the Scriptures, and unto that quhilk *Christ Jesus* himselfe did, and commanded to be done. For this is ane thing universallie granted, that the Spirite of God, quhilk is the Spirite of unitie, is in nathing contrarious unto himselfe. Gif then the interpretation, determination, or sentence of ony Doctor, Kirk, or Councell, repugne to the plaine Worde of God, written in ony uther place of the Scripture, it is thing maist certaine, that there is not the true understanding and meaning of the haly Ghaist, although that Councels, Realmes, and Nations have approved and received the same. For we dare non receive or admit ony interpretation quhilk repugnes to ony principall point of our faith, or to ony uther plaine text of Scripture, or zit unto the rule of charitie.

descended from Aaron, and greater numbers followed the scribes, pharisees, and priests, than unfeignedly believed and followed Christ Jesus and His doctrine . . . and yet no man of judgment, we suppose, will hold that any of the forenamed were the Kirk of God. The notes of the true Kirk, therefore, we believe, confess, and avow to be: first, the true preaching of the Word of God, in which God has revealed Himself to us, as the writings of the prophets and apostles declare; secondly, the right administration of the sacraments of Christ Jesus, with which must be associated the Word and promise of God to seal and confirm them in our hearts; and lastly, ecclesiastical discipline uprightly ministered, as God's Word prescribes, whereby vice is repressed and virtue nourished. Then wherever these notes are seen and continue for any time, be the number complete or not, there, beyond any doubt, is the true Kirk of Christ, who, according to His promise, is in its midst. This is not that universal Kirk of which we have spoken before, but particular Kirks, such as were in Corinth, Galatia, Ephesus, and other places where the ministry was planted by Paul and which he himself called Kirks of God. Such Kirks, we the inhabitants of the realm of Scotland confessing Christ Jesus, do claim to have in our cities, towns, and reformed districts because of the doctrine taught in our Kirks, contained in the written Word of God, that is, the Old and New Testaments, in those books which were originally reckoned canonical. We affirm that in these all things necessary to be believed for the salvation of man are sufficiently expressed. The interpretation of Scripture, we confess, does not belong to any private or public person, nor yet to any Kirk for pre-eminence or precedence, personal or local, which it has above others, but pertains to the Spirit of God by whom the Scriptures were written. When controversy arises about the right understanding of any passage or sentence of Scripture, or for the reformation of any abuse within the Kirk of God, we ought not so much to ask what men have said or done before us, as what the Holy Ghost uniformly speaks within the body of the Scriptures and what Christ Jesus Himself did and commanded. For it is agreed by all that the Spirit of God, who is the Spirit of unity, cannot contradict Himself. So if the interpretation or opinion of any theologian, Kirk, or council, is contrary to the plain Word of God written in any other passage of the Scripture, it is most certain that this is not the true understanding and meaning of the Holy Ghost, although councils, realms, and nations have approved and received it. We dare not receive or admit any interpretation which is contrary to any principal point of our faith, or to any other plain text of Scripture, or to the rule of love.

ARTICLE XIX

OF THE AUTHORITIE OF THE SCRIPTURES

As we beleeve and confesse the Scriptures of God sufficient to instruct and make the man of God perfite, so do we affirme and avow the authoritie of the same to be of God, and nether to depend on men nor angelis. We affirme, therefore, that sik as allege the Scripture to have na uther authoritie bot that quhilk it hes received from the Kirk, to be blasphemous against God, and injurious to the trew Kirk, quhilk alwaies heares and obeyis the voice of her awin Spouse and Pastor; bot takis not upon her to be maistres over the samin.

ARTICLE XX

OF GENERALL COUNCELLIS, OF THEIR POWER,

AUTHORITIE, AND CAUSE OF THEIR CONVENTION

As we do not rashlie damne that quhilk godly men, assembled togither in generall Councel lawfully gathered, have proponed unto us; so without just examination dare we not receive quhatsoever is obtruded unto men under the name of generall Councelis: For plaine it is, as they wer men, so have some of them manifestlie erred, and that in matters of great weight and importance. So farre then as the councell previs the determination and commandement that it gives bee the plaine Worde of God, so soone do we reverence and imbrace the same. Bot gif men, under the name of a councel, pretend to forge unto us new artickles of our faith, or to make constitutionis repugning to the Word of God; then utterlie we must refuse the same as the doctrine of Devils, quhilk drawis our saules from the voyce of our onlie God to follow the doctrines and constitutions of men. The cause then quhy that generall Councellis convened, was nether to make ony perpetual Law, quhllk God before had not maid, nether zit to forge new Artickles of our beleife, nor to give the Word of God authoritie; meikle les to make that to be his Word, or zit the trew interpretation of the same, quhilk wes not before be his haly will expressed in his Word: Bot the cause of Councellis (we meane of sik as merite the name of Councellis) wes partlie for confutation of heresies, and for giving publick confession of their faith to the posteritie of Goddis written Word, and not by ony opinion or prerogative that they culd not erre, be reasson of their generall assemblie: And this we judge to have bene the chiefe cause of general Councellis. The uther wes for gude policie, and ordour to be constitute and observed in the Kirk, quhilk, as in the house of God, is becummis *al things to be done decently and in ordour*. Not that we think that any policie and an ordour in ceremonies can be appoynted for al ages, times, and places: For as ceremonies, sik as men have devised, ar bot temporall; so may and aucht they to be changed, when they rather foster superstition then that they edifie the Kirk using the same.

CHAPTER XIX

THE AUTHORITY OF THE SCRIPTURES

As we believe and confess the Scriptures of God sufficient to instruct and make perfect the man of God, so do we affirm and avow their authority to be from God, and not to depend on men or angels. We affirm, therefore, that those who say the Scriptures have no other authority save that which they have received from the Kirk are blasphemous against God and injurious to the true Kirk, which always hears and obeys the voice of her own Spouse and Pastor, but takes not upon her to be mistress over the same.

CHAPTER XX

GENERAL COUNCILS, THEIR POWER, AUTHORITY,

AND THE CAUSE OF THEIR SUMMONING

As we do not rashly condemn what good men, assembled together in General Councils lawfully gathered, have set before us; so we do not receive uncritically whatever has been declared to men under the name of the General Councils, for it is plain that, being human, some of them have manifestly erred, and that in matters of great weight and importance. So far then as the Council confirms its decrees by the plain Word of God, so far do we reverence and embrace them. But if men, under the name of a Council, pretend to forge for us new articles of faith, or to make decisions contrary to the Word of God, then we must utterly deny them as the doctrine of devils, drawing our souls from the voice of the one God to follow the doctrines and teachings of men. The reason why the General Councils met was not to make any permanent law which God had not made before, nor yet to form new articles for our belief, nor to give the Word of God authority; much less to make that to be His Word, or even the true interpretation of it, which was not expressed previously by His holy will in His Word; but the reason for Councils, at least of those that deserve that name, was partly to refute heresies, and to give public confession of their faith to the generations following, which they did by the authority of God's written Word, and not by any opinion or prerogative that they could not err by reason of their numbers. This, we judge, was the primary reason for General Councils. The second was that good policy and order should be constituted and observed in the Kirk where, as in the house of God, it becomes all things to be done decently and in order. Not that we think any policy or order of ceremonies can be appointed for all ages, times, and places; for as ceremonies which men have devised are but temporal, so they may, and ought to be changed, when they foster superstition rather than edify the Kirk.

ARTICLE XXI
OF THE SACRAMENTIS

As the Fatheris under the Law, besides the veritie of the Sacrifices, had twa chiefe Sacramentes, to wit, Circumcision and the Passeover, the despisers and contemners whereof were not reputed for Gods people; sa so we acknowledge and confesse that we now in the time of the Evangell have twa chiefe Sacramentes, onelie instituted be the Lord *Jesus*, and commanded to be used of all they that will be reputed members of his body, to wit, Baptisme and the Supper or Table of the Lord *Jesus*, called the Communion of his Body and his Blude. And thir Sacramentes, as weil of Auld as of New Testament, now instituted of God, not onelie to make ane visible difference betwix this people and they that wes without his league: Bot also to exerce the faith of his Children, and, be participation of the same Sacramentes, to seill in their hearts the assurance of his promise, and of that most blessed conjunction, union and societie, quhilk the elect have with their head *Christ Jesus*. And this we utterlie damne the vanitie of thay that affirme Sacramentes to be nathing ellis bot naked and baire signes. No, wee assuredlie beleeve that be Baptisme we ar ingrafted in *Christ Jesus*, to be made partakers of his justice, be quhilk our sinnes ar covered and remitted. And alswa, that in the Supper richtlie used, *Christ Jesus* is so joined with us, that hee becummis very nurishment and fude of our saules. Not that we imagine anie transubstantiation of bread into *Christes* body, and of wine into his naturall blude, as the *Papistes* have perniciouslie taucht and damnablie beleeved; bot this unioun and conjunction, quhilk we have with the body and blude of *Christ Jeses* in the richt use of the Sacraments, wrocht be operatioun of the haly Ghaist, who by trew faith carryis us above al things that are visible, carnal, and earthly, and makes us to feede upon the body and blude of *Christ Jesus*, quhilk wes anes broken and shed for us, quhilk now is in heaven, and appearis in the presence of his Father for us: And zit notwithstanding the far distance of place quhilk is betwixt his body now glorified in heaven and us now mortal in this eird, zit we man assuredly beleve that the bread quhil wee break, is the communion of *Christes* bodie, and the cupe quhilk we blesse, is the communion of his blude. So that we confesse, and undoubtedlie beleeve, that the faithfull, in the richt use of the Lords Table, do so eat the bodie and drinke the blude of the Lord *Jesus*, that he remaines in them, and they in him: Zea, they are maid flesh of his flesh, and bone of his bones; that as the eternall God-head hes given to the flesh of *Christ Jesus* (quhilk of the awin conditioun and nature wes mortal and corruptible) life and immortalitie; so dois *Christ Jesus* his flesh and blude eattin and drunkin be us, give unto us the same prerogatives. Quhilk, albeit we confesse are nether given unto us at that time onelie, nether zit be the proper power and vertue of the Sacrament onelie; zit we affirme that the faithfull, in the richt use of the Lords Table, hes conjunction with *Christ Jesus*, as the naturall man can not apprehend: Zea, and farther we affirme, that albeit the faithfull, oppressed be negligence

CHAPTER XXI
THE SACRAMENTS

As the fathers under the Law, besides the reality of the sacrifices, had two chief sacraments, that is, circumcision and the passover, and those who rejected these were not reckoned among God's people; so do we acknowledge and confess that now in the time of the Gospel we have two chief sacraments, which alone were instituted by the Lord Jesus and commanded to be used by all who will be counted members of His body, that is, Baptism and the Supper or Table of the Lord Jesus, also called the Communion of His Body and Blood. These sacraments, both of the Old Testament and of the New, were instituted by God not only to make a visible distinction between His people and those who were without the Covenant, but also to exercise the faith of His children and, by participation of these sacraments, to seal in their hearts the assurance of His promise, and of that most blessed conjunction, union, and society, which the chosen have with their Head, Christ Jesus. And so we utterly condemn the vanity of those who affirm the sacraments to be nothing else than naked and bare signs. No, we assuredly believe that by Baptism we are engrafted into Christ Jesus, to be made partakers of His righteousness, by which our sins are covered and remitted, and also that in the Supper rightly used, Christ Jesus is so joined with us that He becomes the very nourishment and food of our souls. Not that we imagine any transubstantiation of bread into Christ's body, and of wine into His natural blood, as the Romanists have perniciously taught and wrongly believed; but this union and conjunction which we have with the body and blood of Christ Jesus in the right use of the sacraments is wrought by means of the Holy Ghost, who by true faith carries us above all things that are visible, carnal, and earthly, and makes us feed upon the body and blood of Christ Jesus, once broken and shed for us but now in heaven, and appearing for us in the presence of His Father. Notwithstanding the distance between His glorified body in heaven and mortal men on earth, yet we must assuredly believe that the bread which we break is the communion of Christ's body and the cup which we bless the communion of His blood. Thus we confess and believe without doubt that the faithful, in the right use of the Lord's Table, do so eat the body and drink the blood of the Lord Jesus that He remains in them and they in Him; they are so made flesh of His flesh and bone of His bone that as the eternal Godhood has given to the flesh of Christ Jesus, which by nature was corruptible and mortal, life and immortality, so the eating and drinking of the flesh and blood of Christ Jesus does the like for us. We grant that this is neither given to us merely at the time nor by the power and virtue of the sacrament alone, but we affirm that the faithful, in the right use of the Lord's Table, have such union with Christ Jesus as the natural man cannot apprehend. Further we affirm that although the faithful, hindered by negligence and human weakness, do not profit as much as they ought in the actual moment of the Supper, yet afterwards it shall bring forth fruit, being living seed sown and manlie infirmitie, dois not profite sameikle as they wald, in the verie instant action of the Supper; zit sall it after bring frute furth, as livelie seid sawin in gude ground. For the haly Spirite, quhilk can never be divided fra the richt institution of the Lord *Jesus*, wil not frustrat the faithfull of the fruit of that mysticall action: Bot all thir, we say, cummis of trew faith, quhilk apprehendis *Christ Jesus*, who only makis this Sacrament effectuall unto us. And therefore, whosoever sclanders us, as that we affirme or beleeve Sacraments to be naked and bair Signes, do injurie unto us, and speaks against the manifest trueth. Bot this liberallie and franklie we confesse, that we make ane distinctioun betwixt *Christ Jesus* in his eternall substance, and betwixt the Elements of the Sacramentall Signes. So that wee will nether worship the Signes, in place of that quhilk is signified be them, nether zit doe we despise, and interpret them as unprofitable and vaine, bot do use them with all reverence, examining our selves diligentlie before that so we do; because we are assured be the mouth of the Apostle, *That sik as eat of that bread, and drink of that coup unworthelie, are guiltie of the bodie and blude of* Christ Jesus.

in good ground; for the Holy Spirit, who can never be separated from the right institution of the Lord Jesus, will not deprive the faithful of the fruit of that mystical action. Yet all this, we say again, comes of that true faith which apprehends Christ Jesus, who alone makes the sacrament effective in us. Therefore, if anyone slanders us by saying that we affirm or believe the sacraments to be symbols and nothing more, they are libellous and speak against the plain facts. On the other hand we readily admit that we make a distinction between Christ Jesus in His eternal substance and the elements of the sacramental signs. So we neither worship the elements, in place of that which they signify, nor yet do we despise them or undervalue them, but we use them with great reverence, examining ourselves diligently before we participate, since we are assured by the mouth of the apostle that 'whosoever shall eat this bread, and drink this cup of the Lord, unworthily, shall be guilty of the body and blood of the Lord'.

ARTICLE XXII

OF THE RICHT ADMINISTRATIOUN OF THE SACRAMENTS

That Sacramentis be richtlie ministrat, we judge twa things requisite: The ane, that they be ministrat be lauchful Ministers, whom we affirme to be only they that ar appoynted to the preaching of the word, into quhais mouthes God hes put sum Sermon of exhortation, they being men lauchfullie chosen thereto be sum Kirk. The uther, that they be ministrat in sik elements, and in sik sort, as God hes appointed; else, we affirme, that they cease to be the richt Sacraments of *Christ Jesus*. And therefore it is that we flee the doctrine of the *Papistical* Kirk, in participatioun of their sacraments; first, because their Ministers are na Ministers of *Christ Jesus*; zea (quhilk is mair horrible) they suffer wemen, whome the haly Ghaist will not suffer to teache in the Congregatioun, to baptize: And secundly, because they have so adulterate both the one Sacrament and the uther with their awin inventions, that no part of *Christs* action abydes in the originall puritie: For Oyle, Salt, Spittill, and sik lyke in Baptisme, ar bot mennis inventiounis. Adoration, Veneration, bearing throw streitis and townes, and keiping of bread in boxis or buistis, ar prophanatioun of *Christs* Sacramentis, and na use of the same: For *Christ Jesus* saide, *Take, eat*, &c., *do ze this in remembrance of me*. Be quhilk words and charge he sanctifyed bread and wine, to the Sacrament of his halie bodie and blude, to the end that the ane suld be eaten, and that all suld drinke of the uther, and not that thay suld be keiped to be worshipped and honoured as God, as the *Papistes* have done heirtofore. Who also committed Sacrilege, steilling from the people the ane parte of the Sacrament, to wit, the blessed coupe. Moreover, that the Sacramentis be richtlie used, it is required, that the end and cause why the Sacramentis were institute, be understood and

CHAPTER XXII

THE RIGHT ADMINISTRATION OF THE SACRAMENTS

Two things are necessary for the right administration of the sacraments. The first is that they should be ministered by lawful ministers, and we declare that these are men appointed to preach the Word, unto whom God has given the power to preach the Gospel, and who are lawfully called by some Kirk. The second is that they should be ministered in the elements and manner which God has appointed. Otherwise they cease to be the sacraments of Christ Jesus. This is why we abandon the teaching of the Roman Church and withdraw from its sacraments; firstly, because their ministers are not true ministers of Christ Jesus (indeed they even allow women, whom the Holy Ghost will not permit to preach in the congregation, to baptize) and, secondly, because they have so adulterated both the sacraments with their own additions that no part of Christ's original act remains in its original simplicity. The addition of oil, salt, spittle, and such like in baptism, are merely human additions. To adore or venerate the sacrament, to carry it through streets and towns in procession, or to reserve it in a special case, is not the proper use of Christ's sacrament but an abuse of it. Christ Jesus said, 'Take ye, eat ye', and 'Do this in remembrance of Me.' By these words and commands He sanctified bread and wine to be the sacrament of His holy body and blood, so that the one should be eaten and that all should drink of the other, and not that they should be reserved for worship or honoured as God, as the Romanists do. Further, in withdrawing one part of the sacrament – the blessed cup – from the people, they have committed sacrilege. Moreover, if the sacraments are to be rightly used it is essential that the end and purpose of their institution should be understood, not only by the minister but by the recipients. For if the recipient

observed, asweil of the minister as of the receiveris: For gif the opinion be changed in the receiver, the richt use ceassis; quhilk is maist evident be the rejection of the sacrifices: As also gif the teacher planely teache fals doctrine, quhilk were odious and abhominable before God (albeit they were his awin ordinance) because that wicked men use them to an uther end than God hes ordaned. The same affirme we of the Sacraments in the *Papistical* kirk; in quhilk, we affirme, the haill action of the Lord *Jesus* to be adulterated, asweill in the external forme, as in the end and opinion. Quhat *Christ Jesus* did, and commanded to be done, is evident be the Evangelistes and be Saint *Paull*: quhat the Preist dois at his altar we neid not to rehearse. The end and cause of Christs institution, and why the selfsame suld be used, is expressed in thir words, *Doe ze this in remembrance of me, als oft as ze sall eit of this bread, and drinke of this coupe, ze sall shaw furth,* that is, extoll, preach, magnifie and praise *the Lords death, till he cum.* Bot to quhat end, and in what opinioun the Preists say their Messe, let the wordes of the same, their awin Doctouris and wryytings witnes: To wit, that they, as Mediatoris betwix *Christ* and his Kirk, do offer unto God the Father, a Sacrifice propitiatorie for the sinnes of the quick and the dead. Quhilk doctrine, as blasphemous to *Christ Jesus*, and making derogation to the sufficiencie of his only Sacrifice, once offered for purgatioun of all they that sall be santifyed, we utterly abhorre, detest and renounce.

does not understand what is being done, the sacrament is not being rightly used, as is seen in the case of the Old Testament sacrifices. Similarly, if the teacher teaches false doctrine which is hateful to God, even though the sacraments are His own ordinance, they are not rightly used, since wicked men have used them for another end than what God commanded. We affirm that this has been done to the sacraments in the Roman Church, for there the whole action of the Lord Jesus is adulterated in form, purpose, and meaning. What Christ Jesus did, and commanded to be done, is evident from the Gospels and from St Paul; what the priest does at the altar we do not need to tell. The end and purpose of Christ's institution, for which it should be used, is set forth in the words, 'Do this in remembrance of Me', and 'For as often as ye eat this bread and drink this cup ye do show' – that is, extol, preach, magnify, and praise – 'the Lord's death, till He come'. But let the words of the mass, and their own doctors and teachings witness, what is the purpose and meaning of the mass; it is that, as mediators between Christ and His Kirk, they should offer to God the Father a sacrifice in propitiation for the sins of the living and of the dead. This doctrine is blasphemous to Christ Jesus and would deprive His unique sacrifice, once offered on the cross for the cleansing of all who are to be sanctified, of its sufficiency; so we detest and renounce it.

Article XXIII
TO WHOME SACRAMENTIS APPERTEINE

We confesse & acknawledge that Baptisme apperteinis asweil to the infants of the faithfull, as unto them that be of age and discretion: And so we damne the error of the *Anabaptists*, who denies baptisme to apperteine to Children, before that they have faith and understanding. Bot the Supper of the Lord, we confesse to appertaine to sik only as be of the houshald of Faith, and can trie and examine themselves, asweil in their faith, as in their dewtie towards their Nichtbouris; sik as eite and drink at that haly Table without faith, or being at dissension and division with their brethren, do eat unworthelie: And therefore it is, that in our Kirk our Ministers tak publick & particular examination, of the knawledge and conversation of sik as are to be admitted to the Table of the Lord *Jesus.*

Chapter XXIII
TO WHOM SACRAMENTS APPERTAIN

We hold that baptism applies as much to the children of the faithful as to those who are of age and discretion, and so we condemn the error of the Anabaptists, who deny that children should be baptized before they have faith and understanding. But we hold that the Supper of the Lord is only for those who are of the household of faith and can try and examine themselves both in their faith and their duty to their neighbours. Those who eat and drink at that holy table without faith, or without peace and goodwill to their brethren, eat unworthily. This is the reason why ministers in our Kirk make public and individual examination of those who are to be admitted to the table of the Lord Jesus.

Article XXIV
OF THE CIVILE MAGISTRATE

We confesse and acknawledge Empyres, Kingdomes, Dominiounis, and Citties to be distincted and ordained be God; the powers and authoritie in the same, be it of Emperours in their Empyres, of Kingis in their Realmes, Dukes and Princes in their Dominionis, and of utheris Magistrates in the Citties, to be Gods haly ordinance, ordained for manifestatioun of his awin glory, and for

Chapter XXIV
THE CIVIL MAGISTRATE

We confess and acknowledge that empires, kingdoms, dominions, and cities are appointed and ordained by God; the powers and authorities in them, emperors in empires, kings in their realms, dukes and princes in their dominions, and magistrates in cities, are ordained by God's holy ordinance for the manifestation of His own glory and for the good and well being of all men.

the singular profite and commoditie of mankind: So that whosoever goeth about to take away, or to confound the haill state of Civile policies, now long established; we affirme the same men not onely to be enimies to mankinde, but also wickedly to fecht against Goddis expressed will. Wee farther confesse and acknawledge, that sik persouns as are placed in authoritie ar to be loved, honoured, feared, and halden in most reverent estimatioun; because that they are the Lieu-tennents of God, in whose Sessiouns God himself dois sit and judge: Zea, even the Judges & Princes themselves, to whome be God is given the sword, to the praise and defence of gude men, and to revenge and punish all open malefactors. Mairover, to Kings, Princes, Rulers and Magistrates, wee affirme that chieflie and most principallie the conservation and purgation of the Religioun apperteinis; so that not onlie they are appointed for Civill policie, bot also for maintenance of the trew Religioun, and for suppressing of Idolatrie and Superstitioun whatsoever: As in *David, Josaphat, Ezechias, Josias*, and utheris highlie commended for their zeale in that caise, may be espyed.

And therefore wee confesse and avow, that sik as resist the supreme power, doing that thing quhilk apperteins to his charge, do resist Goddis ordinance; and therefore cannot be guiltles. And farther we affirme, that whosoever denies unto them ayde, their counsell and comfort, quhiles the Princes and Rulers vigilantly travell in execution of their office, that the same men deny their helpe, support and counsell to God, quha, be the presence of his Lieu-tennent, dois crave it of them.

We hold that any men who conspire to rebel or to overturn the civil powers, as duly established, are not merely enemies to humanity but rebels against God's will. Further, we confess and acknowledge that such persons as are set in authority are to be loved, honoured, feared, and held in the highest respect, because they are the lieutenants of God, and in their councils God Himself doth sit and judge. They are the judges and princes to whom God has given the sword for the praise and defence of good men and the punishment of all open evil doers. Moreover, we state that the preservation and purification of religion is particularly the duty of kings, princes, rulers, and magistrates. They are not only appointed for civil government but also to maintain true religion and to suppress all idolatry and superstition. This may be seen in David, Jehosaphat, Hezekiah, Josiah, and others highly commended for their zeal in that cause.

Therefore we confess and avow that those who resist the supreme powers, so long as they are acting in their own spheres, are resisting God's ordinance and cannot be held guiltless. We further state that so long as princes and rulers vigilantly fulfil their office, anyone who denies them aid, counsel, or service, denies it to God, who by His lieutenant craves it of them.

Article XXV

OF THE GUIFTES FREELY GIVEN TO THE KIRK

Albeit that the Worde of God trewly preached, and the Sacraments richtlie ministred, and Discipline executed according to the Worde of God, be the certaine and infallible Signes of the trew Kirk, we meane not that everie particular persoun joyned with sik company, be ane elect member of *Christ Jesus*: For we acknawledge and confesse, that Dornell, Cockell, and Caffe may be sawen, grow, and in great aboundance lie in the middis of the Wheit, that is, the Reprobate may be joyned in the societie of the Elect, and may externally use with them the benefites of the worde and Sacraments: Bot sik being bot temporall professoures in mouth, but not in heart, do fall backe, and continew not to the end. And therefore have they na fruite of *Christs* death, Resurrection nor Ascension. Bot sik as with heart unfainedly beleeve, and with mouth bauldly confesse the Lord *Jesus*, as before we have said, sall most assuredly receive their guiftes: First, in this life, remission of sinnes, and that be only faith in *Christs* blude; in samekle, that albeit sinne remaine and continuallie abyde in thir our mortall bodies, zit it is not imputed unto us, bot is remitted, and covered with *Christs* justice. Secundly, in the general judgement, there sall be given to every man and woman resurrection of the flesh: For the Sea sall give her dead; the Earth, they

Chapter XXV

THE GIFTS FREELY GIVEN TO THE KIRK

Although the Word of God truly preached, the Sacraments rightly ministered, and discipline executed according to the Word of God, are certain and infallible signs of the true Kirk, we do not mean that every individual person in that company is a chosen member of Christ Jesus. We acknowledge and confess that many weeds and tares are sown among the corn and grow in great abundance in its amidst, and that the reprobate may be found in the fellowship of the chosen and may take an outward part with them in the benefits of the Word and sacraments. But since they only confess God for a time with their mouths and not with their hearts, they lapse, and do not continue to the end. Therefore they do not share the fruits of Christ's death, resurrection, and ascension. But such as unfeignedly believe with the heart and boldly confess the Lord Jesus with their mouths shall certainly receive His gifts. Firstly, in this life, they shall receive remission of sins and that by faith in Christ's blood alone; for though sin shall remain and continually abide in our mortal bodies, yet it shall not be counted against us, but be pardoned, and covered with Christ's righteousness. Secondly, in the general judgment, there shall be given to every man and woman resurrection of the flesh. The seas shall give up her dead, and the earth those who are buried within that therein be inclosed; zea, the Eternall our God sall stretche our his hand on the dust, and the dead sall arise uncorruptible, and that in the substance of the selfe same flesh that every man now beiris, to receive according to their warkis, glory or punishment: For sik as now delyte in vanity, cruelty, filthynes, superstition or Idolatry, sal be adjudged to the fire unquencheable: In quhilk they sall be tormented for ever, asweill in their awin bodyes, as in their saules, quhilk now they give to serve the Devill in all abhomination. Bot sik as continew in weil doing to the end, bauldely professing the Lord *Jesus*, we constantly beleve, that they sall receive glorie, honor, and immortality, to reigne for ever in life everlasting with *Christ Jesus*, to whose glorified body all his Elect sall be made lyke, when he sall appeir againe in judgement, and sall rander up the kingdome to God his father, who then sall bee, and ever sall remaine all in all things God blessed for ever: To whome, with the Sonne and with the haly Ghaist, be all honour and glorie, now and ever. *So be it.*

Arise (O Lord) and let thy enimies be confounded; let them flee from thy presence that hate thy godlie Name. Give thy servands strenth to speake thy word in bauldnesse, and let all Natiouns cleave to thy trew knawledge. Amen.

Thir Acts and Artickles ar red in the face of Parliament, and ratifyed be the thre Estatis, at Edinburgh the 17 day of August, the Zeir of GOD 1560 Zeiris.

her. Yea, the Eternal, our God, shall stretch out His hand on the dust, and the dead shall arise incorruptible, and in the very substance of the selfsame flesh which every man now bears, to receive according to their works, glory or punishment. Such as now delight in vanity, cruelty, filthiness, superstition, or idolatry, shall be condemned to the fire unquenchable, in which those who now serve the devil in all abominations shall be tormented forever, both in body and in spirit. But such as continue in welldoing to the end, boldly confessing the Lord Jesus, shall receive glory, honour, and immortality, we constantly believe, to reign forever in life everlasting with Christ Jesus, to whose glorified body all His chosen shall be made like, when He shall appear again in judgment and shall render up the Kingdom to God His Father, who then shall be and ever shall remain, all in all things, God blessed forever. To whom, with the Son and the Holy Ghost, be all honour and glory, now and ever. Amen.

Arise, O Lord, and let Thine enemies be confounded; let them flee from Thy presence that hate Thy godly Name. Give Thy servants strength to speak Thy Word with boldness, and let all nations cleave to the true knowledge of Thee. Amen.

These Acts and articles were read in the face of the Parliament and ratified by the Three Estates, at Edinburgh the 17 day of August, the year of God 1560 years.

INDEX